John Scally

Odd Balls

THE FUNNY SIDE OF RUGBY

CURRACH
PRESS

First published in 2015 by
CURRACH PRESS
55A Spruce Avenue,
Stillorgan Industrial Park,
Blackrock, Co. Dublin

Cover design by sin é design
Origination by Currach Press
Printed by ScandBook AB, Sweden

ISBN 978 1 78218 843 8

Contents

Acknowledgements

Thanks to Emma Spence for her ongoing support. When I asked her about dedicating this book to her brother Nevin, who died in such tragic circumstances in 2012, she told me that it was appropriate because 'Nevin was famous in the Ulster squad for telling the silliest jokes.'

This book is only possible because of the great generosity of so many players of the past and present, too many to mention, who have shared their time and funny stories with me over the years. Sadly, some of them have left us for the great rugby pitch in the sky, including the peerless Jack Kyle, Moss Keane, Mick Doyle, Tom Rooney, Des O'Brien, Bill McLaren, Ray Gravell and Jim McCarthy.

As this book was in its beginnings, I was shocked and saddened to hear of the death of a great out-half, Ian Burns.

The one and only Mick Quinn has always held a special place in my affections because of his willingness to share his treasure trove of stories with me. I am also very grateful to Ken Ging because of his vast reservoir of funny stories.

The names Tony Ward and Ollie Campbell are inescapably intertwined in Irish rugby history, but for me they fall into the category of 'very special friends'.

My good friend Pat Spillane is perhaps an unlikely contributor to this book. I am grateful to him for his homage to Mick Doyle. I am also indebted to the incredibly thoughtful Joe Schmidt for past kindnesses. Likewise Willie Anderson, Nigel Carr, David Irwin and Philip Rainey have also been very helpful to me.

Thanks to Patrick, Michael and all at Currach Press.

INTRODUCTION

The Kick-Off

According to the man who knows everything – I of course refer to Eamon Dunphy – rugby is the new sex.

The task I set myself in this book was to pay homage to the characters of Irish rugby and to write an entertaining book. In addition, I wanted to honour some of the Irish players who have attained legendary status more for their activities off the pitch than for anything they ever did on it. Were I to include all the players in the latter category this book would have more chapters than the Bible! This does mean that some of the stories told in the book are more folklore than fact, though the majority are based on the recollections of players of the past and present in conversations with me.

If laughter be the food of rugby, play on. If you didn't have humour, you couldn't have rugby, given the often fluctuating fortunes of every team in the world. This book also serves a serious purpose. It proves beyond reasonable doubt the sociological truth that the relationship between the English and the rest of the rugby world is based on trust and understanding: they don't trust us and we don't understand them.

On the World Cup and Grand Slam index Ireland does not feature very prominently. Yet no student of the game would disagree that Ireland has given international rugby a disproportionate number of the great characters of the game. In this category are people like Jack MacCaulay. He was said to be the first married man to be capped in international rugby in 1887 – according to rugby folklore, he got married just to get a leave of absence to play for Ireland.

In theory, the rugby field is a stage on which the players attempt to establish their superior skills. In practice, it is often the forum where an engaging battle of wits can occur, with the battle on the scoreboard the last thing on anyone's mind. Sometimes the results are bemusing. More often, as we shall see, they are amusing. This collection reveals the unquenchable, insatiable wit that smoulders unseen under the mute, impassive faces of the world's toughest men. The result is a wry, idiosyncratic and sometimes bizarre catalogue of comic creations.

To quote Groucho Marx: 'These are my principles, and if you don't like them ... well, I have others.'

CHAPTER ONE

The Strife of Brian

'They call him God. Well I reckon he's a much better player than that.' Thus spoke Stuart Barnes during the Sky Sports commentary of one of the greatest tries of all time. In his first Test for the Lions in 2001, Brian O'Driscoll left the World Champions, Australia, looking as slow as growing grass as he ran half the field and scythed through their defence to score one of the greatest individual tries ever seen, the very signature of genius. Following his vintage displays for the Lions, Brian continued his dizzying ascent to become one of the biggest names in world rugby. The French rugby legend Philippe Sella said of him, 'Brian is like a locomotive.' Tony Ward frequently refers to him as 'he who walks on water'. He is to the rugby aficionado what Nureyev is to the ballet enthusiast. Fear can keep you a prisoner; hope can set you free. From his earliest days O'Driscoll approached each international as if he expected to win, regardless of the opposition. This can-do philosophy was a breath of fresh air to Irish rugby.

This chapter is devoted to the so-called 'golden generation' of Irish rugby.

THE FRUIT OF WISDOM

Bod was once dared by Gordon D'Arcy to say something unusual in a press conference. The rugby media were a bit taken aback when, in the middle of a press conference, O'Driscoll responded to a question with: 'Knowledge is knowing a tomato is a fruit but wisdom is knowing not to put it into a fruit salad.'

Even in retirement Brian O'Driscoll cannot resist winding up his former teammates. After Ireland beat France in 2015 he tweeted: 'Massive back line we have since they got rid of the midgets huh @Gordonwdarcy?!' Darcy struck back immediately: '@BrianODriscoll yep serious units. Thank God I've got 2 inches on you #briankingofthemidgets.'

BUM DEAL

Sometimes teammates just don't get each other. It is probably safe to assume that Jason McAteer and Roy Keane were never going to be soulmates given the difference in their personalities.

Jason was lounging around the Ireland team hotel when Roy laid into him about being too unfocused.

Jason said: 'I go with the flow.'

Roy gave him a withering look before saying: 'Do you know what else goes with the flow?'

Jason blinked and said: 'I don't know.'

Roy replied scathingly: 'Dead fish.'

Denis Hickie and Brian O'Driscoll had a very different type of relationship. Prop forwards are generally a more rotund breed than backs – consequently, when you want to insult a back you say he looks like a prop forward. Tony O'Reilly famously said: 'Prop forwards don't get Valentine cards for religious reasons – God made them ugly.'

Hickie was attending a wedding and saw Bod in the distance, at a time when Drico was carrying a few extra pounds, and waspishly remarked: 'I didn't know Paul Wallace (prop forward with the Lions in South Africa in 1997) was coming to the wedding.'

HAIR-RAISING

Hickie and O'Driscoll enjoyed a good-natured rivalry as they yo-yoed in the race to become Ireland's record-breaking try scorer. O'Driscoll grabbed the record off Hickie with his twenty-fourth try for Ireland against Italy in 2004. After the match Drico received a text message from Hickie: 'I suppose I should maybe, perhaps, congratulate you on your new record. Bo***cks!'

DO YOU THINK I'M SEXY?

On legal advice, what Ronan O'Gara said to Bod after he went on *The Late Late Show* to talk about being voted Ireland's sexiest man cannot be repeated in these pages. Likewise, if the exact words Peter Clohessy used when he saw Drico had dyed his hair blonde were printed here, this book would need an XXX rating.

PUTTING YOUR FOOT IN IT

In 2005 Clive Woodward decided to employ Tony Blair's 'spin doctor' Alastair Campbell as the team's press officer. After the infamous spear tackle ruled O'Driscoll out after the first minute of the first Test, the captaincy was handed to Gareth 'Alfie' Thomas. At one point Tony Blair rang Campbell and wanted to wish Alfie well. When Campbell passed him the phone the Prime Minister said: 'Hi, it's Tony.'

Thomas blurts out: 'Tony who?'

When he sees Campbell's reaction he immediately becomes aware of his error and attempts to undo the damage by saying: 'Oh for f**k's sake. I'm so sorry, sir.'

At one point on the tour Donncha O'Callaghan yanked down Campbell's trousers from behind. As he frantically tried to cover up his Burnley FC boxer shorts, he did not notice his mobile phone drop out of his pocket. Steve Thompson, the English hooker, took it away from him and the entire squad later tried to send a love message to Tony Blair. When they couldn't find the PM's number, everyone in his address book was sent an 'I love you' message.

In bod we trust

On the Lions tour to South Africa in 2009, Brian fell into a swimming pool and was fined £25 by the players' court. Tour judge Alun Wyn Jones remarked: 'Brian is a great player, but I can confirm he can't walk on water.'

Leaving on a jetplane

At the height of the rivalry between Ronan O'Gara and Johnny Sexton rumours went around that there was a terrible plane crash. According to folklore, Brian O'Driscoll went up to Sexton and said: 'I've got good news and bad news. Which do you want first?'

'Give us the bad news.'

'A plane has gone down killing a hundred people.'

'Oh my God that's awful. What's the good news?'

'Ronan O'Gara was on it.'

Play it forward

A legend of Irish rugby claims that Brian O'Driscoll's favourite joke is: What do you call those types of people who constantly hang around rugby players, follow them to cool places and generally idolise their every move?

Forwards.

The Princes of Wales

Such was the Welsh dominance of the Lions third Test team in 2013 that Johnny Sexton joked that it was a matter of enormous pride to him to have finally made his Welsh international debut.

Warren Gatland's sensational decision to drop O'Driscoll for that game was the main talking point. Despite the controversy of being dropped for the final Test, Drico had some sweet moments after the game. He was able to bring his baby daughter Sadie onto the pitch. Then he met James Bond himself when Daniel Craig went into the Lions' changing room. The bad pun police were called when someone suggested Drico was in 'Double-O-Heaven.'

Weeks after the tour, Drico told Shane Horgan in a TV interview that Warren Gatland would not be on his Christmas card list after he dropped him. O'Driscoll's comments got huge media attention, and shortly afterwards he realised that he was going to have to meet Gatland at a function. Not wishing the 'feud' to develop further, O'Driscoll took the wind out his coach's sails by presenting him with a Christmas card – even though it was only September.

RADIO GA-GA

After the Lions tour, Drico went into a hi-tech electrical store to buy a car radio and the salesman said, 'This is the very latest model. It's voice-activated. You just tell it what you want to listen to and the station changes automatically. There's no need to take your hands off the wheel.'

On the way home Drico decided to test it. He said, 'Classical' and the sound of the RTÉ orchestra filled the car. He said, 'Country' and instantly he was listening to Dolly Parton. Then suddenly a pedestrian stepped off the pavement in front of him, causing him to swerve violently and shout at him, 'F**king idiot.' Then the radio changed to a documentary on Warren Gatland.

REVENGE IS SWEET

Gatland's decision to drop Drico immediately put the focus on Ireland's next game against Wales. Ireland's call was answered with a resounding 26–3 win. *The Sunday Independent* had the best take on it with their headline: 'Wales left to sink up Schmidt creek.'

Joe Schmidt was the one man who could pop Drico's bubble. During his time as Leinster coach, Joe was doing video analysis and reached a point where Bod and Gordon D'Arcy had butchered a try-scoring opportunity – D'Arcy had given a poor pass and O'Driscoll could not hold onto it. Joe first asked D'Arcy what he thought. 'It was a poor pass,' he replied.

Then he turned to Drico who answered: 'It was a bit low for me.'

Bod quickly realised that he was in fact the target when Schmidt asked him: 'Do you think a world class player should have caught it?'

All Drico could do was meekly reply: 'A world class player should have caught it.'

SNAKES ALIVE

On the 2001 Lions tour to Australia, four of the squad – Rob Howley, Derek Quinnell, Dafydd James and Brian O'Driscoll – went to a zoo and were shown a snake. The snake handler explained: 'This is a 25 ft Asian Python. This type of snake is capable of eating goats, lambs and is reputed to have eaten humans as well.' The four brave Lions were ready to beat a hasty retreat when a photographer working with the Lions came up: 'Right lads, let's have a picture, all four of you holding the snake. No getting out of it, you're all doing it.'

Realising that they had to have their photo taken, Quinnell immediately rushed forward and grabbed hold of the snake's tail. Howley and O'Driscoll copped on immediately and stepped smartly forward. James couldn't fathom why his three friends were suddenly keen to embrace this huge great snake. It was too late when he twigged what was going on. O'Driscoll and Howley had grabbed the middle section of the snake, and there was only one place left for James in the photo. He had to hold the python by its head, flicking tongue and gleaming eyes. The photo showed three happy Lions and one looking absolutely terrified.

GROANER

After the tour, Jonny Wilkinson described O'Driscoll as 'the Monica Seles of table tennis. You've never heard grunting like it'.

THE LIFE OF BRIAN

O'Driscoll has been in thrall to the game of rugby for as long as he can remember. It helps that his father, Frank, played for Ireland and that his cousins Barry and John also played for their country.

Ours is an age wedded to an almost mystical concept of celebrity. Brian's mother, Geraldine, is all too aware of this. The France game in 2000, when Bod scored the three tries, changed everything for Brian; and indeed for his family. Geraldine first realised this when she was introduced to someone after the match and they said, 'This is Geraldine O'Driscoll. She used to be Frank O'Driscoll's wife. Now she's Brian O'Driscoll's mother.'

That famous game was on a Sunday, and shortly after the match Frank and Geraldine had to rush for the train to get home for work the next day. One of their daughters was in Australia at the time and she rang them on her mobile. She said, 'Mum, after Brian's three tries I'm a minor celebrity here now.'

Geraldine saw just how famous Brian had become the following Halloween. She knew there would be lots of kids calling to the house trick-or-treating. She put piles of sweets on the table and left Brian in charge of them. When she came back she was shocked to find all the sweets still there, with a bundle of pieces of paper lying beside them. She asked Brian what had happened and he replied, 'The doorbell hasn't stopped ringing all evening but none of the kids want the sweets. They just want my autograph.'

HOLY SMOKES

Everybody loves a winner. In 2001, the Irish rugby team got an audience with the Pope when they travelled to Rome to play Italy. Injury forced O'Driscoll to miss the trip. Pope John Paul II was said to be still eagerly awaiting his audience with Brian O'Driscoll on his deathbed.

THE WRITE STUFF

The publishing event of the year in Irish rugby circles in 2014 was the launch of Brian O'Driscoll's autobiography. Unfortunately for Brian, the book was somewhat overshadowed by the controversies created by both Roy Keane's and Kevin Pietersen's books. *The Irish Independent* tried to come to his rescue by its summary of Keano's book: 'Roy has a lot of rows, swears a lot, sees another player eating crisps, has a big beard – and, em, that's about it.'

Drico was moved to tweet: 'I reckon my book is going to read something from Enid Blyton in comparison to KP & Keano's!!! #onlyjokingRogisatranny.'

DOING IT BY THE BOOK

After O'Driscoll published his autobiography, much of the press interest was generated by the fact that he had once been arrested in America. Mario Rosenstock did a sketch on the *Ian Dempsey Breakfast Show* on Today FM.

They changed *The Shawshank Redemption* to *The Bodshank Redemption*. In prison, Bod regales his fellow prisoners with tales of his many dealings with a strange breed of 'hookers' and of the hardest man he knows, Paulie, who goes out to 'take peoples' heads off'.

In the original film, the hero puts up a poster of Rita Hayworth and escapes by digging a hole in the wall behind the picture. In the remake, Bod puts up a poster of Ollie Campbell and escapes 'through Ollie Campbell's hole'.

Ruck and rollers

Brian O'Driscoll came before God at the throne of Heaven with Ronan O'Gara and Tommy Bowe. God said to them, 'Before granting you a place at my side, I must ask for your beliefs.'

Rog stared God directly in the eye and said, 'I believe rugby is the meaning of life. Nothing else has brought so much joy to so many. I have devoted my life to spreading the gospel of rugby.'

God was moved by his passion and eloquence and said, 'You are a man of true faith. Sit by me at my right hand.'

He then turned to Monaghan's most famous rugby son, 'Now, my child tell me what you believe in?'

Bowe answered, 'I believe courage, bravery, loyalty, teamwork, dedication and commitment are the soul of life, and I dedicated my career to living up to those ideals.'

God replied, 'You have spoken well my child. Sit by me at my left hand.'

Then he turned to Bod, 'And you, Mr O'Driscoll, what is that you believe?'

Drico gave him a withering look and replied, 'I believe you are sitting in my chair.'

Time to say goodbye?

When Drico was appointed captain of Ireland for the first time, he was congratulated by his predecessor, Keith Wood. The hooker wished Bod the best of luck and ushered him aside, 'Just a little advice; as tradition goes from one outgoing Ireland captain to the next, take these.'

He handed him three envelopes.

'If you fail to lead Ireland to victory,' he said, 'open an envelope, and inside you will find some invaluable advice as to how to proceed.'

Immediately after Drico's first defeat he remembered Wood's envelopes and opened the first one. 'Blame the referee,' it said.

He walked confidently into the press conference and said, 'Well, there wasn't much between the teams really. In a match like that small mistakes can change the complexion of the game completely, and in that respect I felt that the ref made some decisions that went against us which had a big bearing on the final outcome.'

The journalists nodded wisely. Wood's advice was working well.

Another defeat quickly followed. Bad news, Drico would have to use the second of the three envelopes.

'Blame the place-kicker,' it said. Off the captain went to face the media.

'Well. I thought it was nip and tuck, we had them under pressure, but unfortunately Rog didn't have the best of days with the old shooting boots and so the chances slipped away.'

Again the journalists seemed satisfied with his response. Thank God for these get-out-of-jail-free envelopes, Drico reflected.

His third defeat. Bod was heartbroken, and absolutely gutted not to have won. There was only one consolation – help was at hand. He walked into the dressing room, looking forward to some first-class advice from the third and last envelope. He rummaged in his bag, pulled it out and tore it open. The advice was simple: 'Start writing out three new envelopes.'

PENNEY FOR YOUR THOUGHTS

It is important to have light moments on a tour, whether it is with club, country or the Lions. One effort to break the monotony of a rugby tour is 'a court session', where players are judged by their peers and given an appropriate punishment for their transgressions.

This is good – though not always innocent – fun, and generally involves a fair bit of alcohol. This institution of the rugby tour greatly improves team morale.

People are fined for different reasons, and the more fines they get the more alcohol they enjoy. Players are charged for incidents in training or in matches; for example, somebody who dropped the ball a few times in training might be charged as a 'butterfingers', and their fine might be to drink a bottle of beer without using their hands.

Former England prop Paul Rendall was known as 'Judge' from his days dispensing justice in a players' court. On a tour of Australia, he famously sentenced the team manager Geoff Cooke to eat a daffodil sandwich. Jason Leonard once asked: 'Judge, why don't you have a nickname?' Rendall took him aside and said: 'No one minds you making a complete tool of yourself every now and again, but for God's sake don't let the backs hear you say things like that. You're a forward, and stupid comments are for backs only.'

On the 2013 Lions tour it was Rob Kearney who was in charge of punishments.

The three quietest players in the squad Toby Faletau, Manu Tuilagi and Mako Vunipola were forced to tell the squad a joke on the bus to training every day. No matter how good their joke was, nothing was as funny as watching their pain and mortification.

Kearney devised a game based on rolling a dice and the punishment was determined by the number. Anyone who got a one had to dance for thirty seconds, with no accompanying music, in front of the entire squad. A two granted a player a get-out-of-jail-free card and he passed the dice to somebody else. It was a three that made the Lions' marketing director Charlie McEwen have his head completely shaved. Both Sam Warburton and Warren Gatland threw fives and were left behind after training. The number six involved spending a night sleeping with the kit man. Andy Irvine had that experience.

The biggest laugh though was reserved for Simon Zebo. When he threw a four, his punishment was to ring his then Munster coach Rob Penney and explain, with the entire Lions squad listening, why he should be made Munster captain for the following season.

Penney intuitively knew it was some sort of wind-up and gamely promised to give the suggestion serious consideration.

I, KEANO

As part of his attempts to learn about management, Roy Keane spent time with the All Blacks. His stint in New Zealand coincided with the Irish rugby team's tour. At one point, Keano was privy to the New Zealand team's plans for the upcoming Irish game. Their tactics were very simple: target Ronan O'Gara, as defence was seen to be the one weakness in Rog's game. Keano beamed, as he had prearranged to have dinner with Rog that very evening and he could give him a preview.

That evening Keano referred to the fact that he had been at the team meeting, but decided to tantalise his fellow Corkman by not giving any details initially. After a while Rog could take it no more and blurted out: 'Tell me, do they have a special plan for me tomorrow?'

Keano smiled: 'Brace yourself. It's going to be a tough day at the office. They're going to target you non-stop.'

Rog exclaimed: 'I f**king knew it. They always f**king target me.'

EYE OF THE TIGER

One of the defining sporting images of 2001 was that of blood streaming from O'Gara's eye. During the Lions tour that year Duncan McRae had repeatedly beaten him in the left eye during the match against the New South Wales Waratahs with an eleven punch attack. O'Gara's popularity with the squad after the McRae episode was indicated when everyone wanted to go and sort out 'Duncan Disorderly'.

BUM RAP

Rog brought a new dimension to rugby tours on the 2001 Lions tour. Usually punishment at the players court means drinking an evil alcoholic concoction of something that will have the poor unfortunate retching and the rest of the squad in gales of laughter. Another perennial favourite is the 'Circle of Fire' challenge, where toilet paper is rolled up tight, lit with a match, and the unfortunate player has to clench it between his bum cheeks and run the whole way round the room before the flame reaches their skin.

O'Gara devised a new game with the quaint title of 'Red Arse'. His idea was that there would be one bat at each end of the table and the players had to keep a rally going while running around the table, taking it in turns to hit the ball. Mess up and you were eliminated. He then added: 'Oh, and by the way the loser gets a whack on the backside with the bat from every other player.'

Jim Telfer, forwards coach on that tour, remarked: 'Convincing your mates to join you on the Lions tour to Australia is the easy bit. Now comes the hard bit: convincing your wives to let you go.'

Not every player is a fan of tours though. When Welsh international Scott Gibbs was asked to explain why he gave up touring he replied: 'I don't want to be institutionalised in a hotel, singing stupid songs and showing my arse to all and sundry.'

DIRTY JOKES

Lions tours in particular are the stuff of legend – as much for their off-field activities as for all the epic games on the field. Particularly for a novice, a Lions tour is a journey into the unknown. One player, who shall remain nameless, on the Lions tour to Australia in 2001 was told he would be 'dirt-tracking', a well-known rugby term for not being in the first team on tour. But rather than being downcast, he was excited by the news, declaring that he loved BMXs and asked where the track was. Another was to learn, much to his embarrassment, that on tour when a player expresses an interest in having a 'blowjob', in this context a blowjob meant a short.

BUSY SCHEDULE

During the Celtic Tiger, it was commonplace for stars of the Irish rugby team to be offered small fortunes to make personal appearances. During the height of the boom, a young lady was given a budget of two thousand euro to promote the opening of a pharmacy in Cork. She decided to spend the entire sum on getting a top name in Irish rugby to open the pharmacy. When she got his number, she rang him and explained what she wanted him to do and the fee she would pay him. The conversation unfolded as follows:

'What did you say your name was again?'

'Mary.'

'Well, it's like this Mary. I wouldn't turn over in the bed for two thousand euro.'

TOUGHER THAN THE REST

Every sport has its hard men. Soccer had Grame Souness. Bob Paisley put it best when he said of Souness: 'Most midfielders are made up of a buzzer, a cruncher and a spreader. This boy is all three.'

The hardest man in the history of rugby has to be Wayne 'Buck' Shelford. The All Black forward and former captain was playing against France, in what became known as the 'Battle of Nantes'. First, he lost three teeth after he was kicked in the face at a ruck. Then he was knocked out cold by a blow to the head. To cap it all off, he had his scrotum ripped open, leaving one of his testicles hanging free. Buck recalled to ESPN: 'It bloody well hurt at the time so I just chucked the old proverbial Jesus water down the shorts to make it feel better. That didn't do a lot, so we just played on. I went off the field with twenty minutes to go not really knowing where I was, let alone what day it was. As history shows, we lost the game, and it was not until I got changed that I realised that my scrotum had been torn, and that the testicle was hanging a good four or five inches out of the scrotum. It was all put into place and stitched up nicely.'

Limerick's favourite son Paul O'Connell must push him a close second. In the first Lions Test in 2013 he broke his arm, but did not come off the pitch. After the match, prop Ben Alexander spoke for all when he said: 'He's just broken his arm. But he got up and packed those last few scrums.'

None of the Munster players take the field with fear but such is the force of Paul O'Connell that when he walks on the pitch it is fear itself that is afraid.

His innate modesty was also revealed when he was asked by this writer if he has any interest in a career in the media after rugby. 'I don't think I have the boyish good lucks for a career as a TV pundit,' was the reply.

THESE MISS YOU NIGHTS

Paul O'Connell was walking down the streets of Limerick when he met a beautiful, blonde woman who was in great distress. He asked her to tell him what was wrong: 'Oh, it's terrible. My husband is spending all our savings going to see Munster play. He thinks about Munster all the time. He likes me but he loves Munster. I gave him an ultimatum: It's Munster or me.'

Paul replied. 'Well that seems perfectly reasonable. I'm sure he will see sense. But why are you crying?'

'Because I'm going to miss him.'

ABSOLUTION

One of the stories told about O'Connell goes back to the aftermath of Ireland's triumph over South Africa in autumn 2004. Before the game, the Springboks coach, Jake White, became the *bête noire* of Irish rugby when he publicly stated that Brian O'Driscoll was the only Irish player who would get into the Springboks side, although he reluctantly conceded that the second rows, Paul O'Connell and Malcolm O'Kelly, would be contenders. How significant were White's comments for the Irish players? O'Connell elaborates: 'We had lost two Test games in South Africa that summer because we didn't do the basics right. We beat them that autumn because of two reasons: we did the basics right and we had special players on the day like 'Shaggy' (Shane Horgan) and Drico who could make ground and put them on the back foot. We were aware of Jake White's comments. We slagged each other about it and made a few jokes. There was no need for Eddie (O'Sullivan) to say anything about it to motivate us. If you can't motivate yourself after someone insults you like that there's something wrong with you.'

According to legend, O'Connell went to confession a month after the game and confessed to the priest, 'I lost my temper and said some bad words to one of my opponents.'

'Ahhh, that's a terrible thing for an Irish international to be doing,' the priest said. He took a piece of chalk and drew a mark across the sleeve of his coat.

'That's not all, Father. I got mad and punched one of my opponents.'

'Saints preserve us!' the priest said, making another chalk mark.

'There's more. As I got out of a ruck, I kicked two of the other team's players in the … in a sensitive area.'

'Oh, Jesus, Mary and Joseph!' the priest wailed, making two more chalk marks on his sleeve. 'Who in the world were we playing when you did these awful things?'

'South Africa.'

'Ah, well,' said the priest, wiping his sleeve, 'boys will be boys.'

GRAND SLAM

In 2009 Ireland won a long overdue Grand Slam, the first victory since 1948. Paul retains a strong affection for the coach Declan Kidney:

'My favourite story about him goes back to 2000, before I joined the Munster squad. On the way to the Heineken Cup final against Northampton, Munster had to play Saracens away. Saracens were a club without a tradition and they brought in marketing people to tell them how to bring in the crowds. One of the things they did was to play the Rocky music whenever there was a fight or a row; when the team came onto the pitch they played the 'A-Team' music; when the opposition came on they played the 'Teddy Bears Picnic'; when the Saracens placekicker faced up to a penalty the crowd put on fez hats and had a little routine to guide the ball over the bar, and the tee came on in a remote controlled car. To play against Saracens you have to face a lot of distractions. Before playing them the Munster squad were watching a Saracens match as part of their video analysis. With about two minutes to go on the video, Declan turned on a ghetto blaster and had the A-Team music blaring, put on his fez hat and started playing with the remote control and the lights. After a minute or so Declan turned off the television, took off his hat and turned off the ghetto blaster, and he asked: "What happened in the last sixty seconds of the Saracens game?"'

Nobody knew because they had all been watching him.

Point made.

Scary sight

Despite his toughness, Paul has had to endure some disturbing experiences in Irish rugby. As Ireland's tour of South Africa in 2004 was coming to an end the squad organised John Hayes' stag party. They dressed John up in a gymslip. The sight of a twenty stone man in a gymslip is one that Paul never wants to see again. Someone arranged for two strippers to come along, but they weren't the stars of the show – Colin Farrell was filming there at the time and he came to join the squad for the party. He was a very sound guy and certainly knew how to have a good time. The squad gathered around in a circle with John in the middle and everyone got to ask Colin a question. Everything was going to plan until Donncha O'Callaghan, as only Donncha can, asked: 'What was it like to be the star of Titanic?' The whole place cracked up and the players nearly fell off their seats laughing.

Memory lapse

It's not surprising that Donncha's adventures from that tour spawned another story. In this account Donncha stayed on afterwards to go on a safari holiday. While there, he came upon an elephant in great pain, with a giant thorn in its foot. Donncha very carefully approached the elephant, and gingerly removed the thorn from its foot. The elephant began to walk away, then turned and stared at Donncha for a full minute, locking eyes with him. The elephant then continued on its way. 'I wonder if I ever saw that elephant again would it remember me?' Donncha mused to himself.

The following Christmas, Donncha was back in Munster at a circus. He noticed that one of the elephants kept looking at him, almost like it knew him. Donncha wondered, 'Could this be that elephant I helped?' He decided to get a closer look. With the elephant still giving him the stare down, Donncha moved in closer, getting right up in front of the elephant. They locked eyes. A knowing look seemed to cross the elephant's face. It reached down, picked O'Callaghan up carefully with its trunk, lifted him high in the air, and threw him with a crash to the ground and stomped him to near death.

Turns out it wasn't that elephant.

A FAUX PAS

Geordan Murphy cringes at one of his earliest memories from his time in Leicester.

'I had a real Homer Simpson moment standing beside this guy at the club one day. I didn't recognise him from Adam, and I asked him if he got a chance to play much rugby at the club. I knew immediately from the way he looked at me that I had said something incredibly stupid. It was the Scottish international Craig Joiner. To complete my shame, when he turned around I saw the word Joiner on the back of his jersey.

'With Leicester there are also great characters and practical jokers. We have a decent spread of them throughout the squad, but it comes as no surprise that Austin Healey comes out tops in this respect. He is always willing to get a laugh, and it is great to have someone like him in the squad because he keeps morale up. Of course, he can rub people up the wrong way and often has done so. He does the craziest things. To give a typical example of an Austin activity, when he was away with the English squad he was bored and decided to liven things up by having a game with the English forward Lewis Moody. They sat about ten feet away from each other with their legs apart and the idea was to throw an orange at each other's groin. The problem for Austin was that he wasn't very good, but Lewis was the world champion.'

Tender moments

Geordan Murphy has many happy memories from his rugby career:

'One of the funniest came before playing a European Cup final with Leicester. In the warm-up before the game I was throwing the ball around. I tried to do a clever dummy pass and ended up firing the ball into one of my teammate's groin. It made me laugh – it made him cry.'

Big Mal

There are many stories in the Irish camp about Malcolm O'Kelly's lack of organisation and his capacity for being late. The standard line was: If you are behind Mal in the airport you have missed your plane.

Dedicated Follower of Fashion

A particular favourite in the squad is about the time when Mal was spotted wearing a black shoe and a brown shoe. When this was discreetly pointed out to O'Kelly he shrugged his shoulders nonchalantly and said: 'Don't worry. That's the new fashion. I've another pair at home exactly like that.'

Money's Too Tight to Mention

Shane Byrne had a reputation in the squad for being 'careful with money'. Hence the joke amongst his former Irish colleagues that he installed double glazing windows in his home so his children wouldn't hear the ice cream van.

Long lasting

The former Leinster manager Ken Ging made a speech at the testimonial dinner to mark Byrne's one hundredth Leinster Cap.

He told the story of two elderly Americans who, against all odds, were found to be alive in a disused Japanese POW camp having been captured during World War II. They first asked, 'How is President Roosevelt?'

'Oh, he died a long time ago.'

'And how is Stalin?'

'Oh, he died a long time ago.'

'Please tell us that Winston Churchill is still alive and well.'

'Alas, I'm afraid he died as well.'

'Tell us, is Shane Byrne still playing for Leinster?'

FROM CLARE TO HERE

Arsenal stars Lukas Podolski and Santi Cazorla posted pictures of themselves armed with hurleys, and sent their best wishes to Clare before the 2013 All-Ireland final: 'Today Santi & me smashed it over the bar. Wristyhurlers.'

The same pair recruited the forty-two million man Mesut Özil to join them in a photo with a poster which stated 'G'wan Munster'. Podolski was wearing a headband with the Munster anthem printed on it: 'Stand Up and Fight.'

Jerry Flannery, former Munster legend, was working as a personal trainer at Arsenal at the time and is believed to be behind both tweets.

THE TULLOW TANK

When the Taoiseach, Enda Kenny, decided it was time to establish an Irish secret service, it was felt they needed someone even tougher than James Bond. Three Irish internationals were interviewed for the job.

First in was Cian Healy. He was told that there was going to be no questions, there was just going to be a test. He was given a gun and told to go in to the room next door and shoot the man inside.

Two minutes later Healy returned and mumbled apologetically: 'I can't kill a man.'

Next in was the giant Devon Toner. The same test and the same result.

The final candidate was Seán O'Brien. Shortly after he entered the room there was an almighty racket. Ten minutes later he came out again looking very sweaty. He said: 'I'm sorry it took me so long. That gun you gave me only had blanks for bullets so I had to beat him to death with the gun.'

SIMPLY SIMON

According to rugby legend, a great Munster out-half was called to a premature death. He was met at the gates of heaven by St Peter. St Peter apologised profusely for bringing the rugby player to his eternal reward at such a young age, but explained that the celestial rugby cup final was taking place and as a manager of one of the teams he needed a star player. The out-half was whisked immediately to the stadium and marvelled at the facilities. Such was the excitement of the occasion that the recently deceased player forgot about his death and played the game of his (eternal) life.

With just two minutes to go, St Peter's side were leading by nineteen points when the giant Munster out-half noticed an athletic sub coming onto the opposition side and, in an accent that was immediately identifiable as Cork, giving out instructions. The new arrival got the ball four times and scored four tries, each more stunning than the last. He did not bother with the conversions but had the game restarted immediately and his team won by a point.

After the game St Peter rushed on to console his dejected star player. The ex-Munster player asked: 'Tell me, when did Simon Zebo die?'

'That's not Simon Zebo. That's God. He just thinks he's Simon Zebo.'

CHAPTER TWO

The Keane Edge

At the top of any roll of honour of the characters in world rugby, is Moss Keane.

Since his capture on 8 February 1983, Shergar has supposedly been a stud in the Middle East, galloping around the Scottish Highlands, peacefully grazing in a Channel Island's meadow, part of the mafia, part of a Kentucky killing and even giving riding lessons to runaway British aristocrat Lord Lucan. Likewise, if even a fraction of the stories about Moss were true he would have needed a brewery of his own to supply him with Guinness, broken down more doors than most people have eaten hot dinners and generally been responsible for extraordinary levels of mirth and mayhem. This chapter is a small tribute to a big legend.

THE LEGEND

The entire Irish nation went into mourning in 2010 with the sad news of Moss' death. Few sports personalities were more loved. Speaking to me about his funeral, his great friend Ollie Campbell observed: 'I've never experienced anything like it. It must have gone on for a few hours. Despite his innate modesty Moss would have loved it. When his wife Anne spoke she received a standing ovation. I thought of the line: "Anyone who lives in the hearts of those they leave behind will never die." Those words could have been written for Moss.'

Anne put Moss' date of birth and death in Roman numerals. While Moss, leaning over the banisters of heaven, would be happy to have people know his age, he would have been even happier if people did not know.

UNDERSTATED

Stories about Moss are more common than showers in April – though few are printable in our politically correct times. Some are even true! Moss had a nice line in self-deprecating humour: 'After I left university I found I had no talent for anything so I joined the civil service. I won fifty-two caps – a lot of them just because they couldn't find anybody else.'

Moss toured with the Lions in New Zealand in 1977. After their second Test victory the Lions threw the party to beat all parties in the team hotel. It was soon discovered that one of their players was missing. According to legend, when everyone else expressed concern about him Moss said he knew exactly where the missing person was – next door with his girlfriend. Moss was dispatched to bring the guilty party back – though given strict instructions not to break down any doors. (His nickname on that tour was 'Rent-a-Storm', so the decree seemed more than justified.) The rest of the squad listened to a slight flurry next door and moments later Moss came through the door with the missing player under his arm, completely naked and squirming like a fish on a hook. Under the other arm he held the player's girlfriend in a similar state of undress and embarrassment. Moss, in his best Kerry accent, boomed out: 'To be sure, did you be wanting the two of them?'

In fairness, Moss did try to keep the players intellectually stimulated on the tour. As he finished his last drink, Moss called for silence in the bar and asked a question: 'Who played soccer for Scotland and cricket for England?' Everyone was left scratching their heads and no one could figure out the answer.

Finally just before he walked out the door Moss answered his own question, 'Denis Law and Ian Botham.'

TABLE MANNERS

Moss made his debut with the Irish team in 1974. It was a culture shock for him on many levels. After training on a Sunday morning the team would retreat to the Saddle Room in the Shelbourne Hotel. There was a set meal: roast beef, a selection of seasonal vegetables and a baked potato done in tinfoil. Barry McGann correctly guessed that Moss would not have experienced anything like this before. He told the rest of the squad not to touch their food until Moss started eating. Moss was totally flummoxed by the tinfoil. He turned it over and poked at it from every angle, but to no avail. He looked around for guidance from his teammates but they had not touched a scrap. Exasperated, he took up the tinfoil in his hand and threw it over his shoulder saying: 'Where I come from we don't eat Easter eggs with roast beef.'

THE FRENCH CONNECTION

On Moss' first cap in Paris, Willie John McBride, sensing that his huge frame needed extra nourishment, took him out for a bag of chips the night before the game. They were coming back to the team hotel via a rough area and one of the locals decided to do the unthinkable and steal the chips from Moss. The Keane edge surfaced immediately and Moss floored him with a right hook. His friends all ganged up on the two Irish players and a brawl broke out. Before long there was a trail of bodies on the ground – all of them French. Within minutes, four gendarmes arrived. Moss explained the situation: 'They started it. They stole my chips.' One of the officers responded: 'Messieurs, we didn't come to arrest you. We came to save the mob.'

BRUISED, BROKEN AND BATTERED

Moss made his debut in the Irish scrum in the cauldron of Parc des Princes in 1974. He was stamped on and was feeling very miserable. Consolation came in the form of his colleague Stewart McKinney, 'Cheer up Moss, it could have been a lot worse. You would have suffered brain damage if you'd been kicked in the arse.'

FATHER AND SON

Moss' father was watching his son playing in Lansdowne Road and confessed to a fellow fan, 'I don't know too much about the rules of rugby.'

His friend said, 'Don't worry, your son knows even less.'

KEEPING EVERYBODY HAPPY

Once, Tony Ward and Mick Quinn both got eighteen points in a final trial for Ireland, but Quinn felt he had outplayed Ward on the day and was feeling pretty good. Later that night, Moss Keane came up to Quinn at the reception and told him that he was the best out-half he had ever played with. Quinn was pretty chuffed with his compliment and told him so. Shortly after, he was going to the toilet and he saw Mossie talking to somebody, but he couldn't make out who it was at first. As he passed them by he realised it was Wardy, and he heard Mossie tell him he was without doubt the finest out-half ever to play for Ireland. Quinn gave him a kick in the backside for his dishonesty. Mossie followed him into the toilet, put his arm around him and said: 'Don't worry Scout. I was only being diplomatic.'

A DOG'S LIFE

Moss once was asked to give an after dinner speech at very short notice. He began by saying that he felt like a dog surrounded by four trees – he didn't have a leg to stand on.

TACTICAL INNOVATION

The definitive verdict on Moss came from Mick Doyle: 'For the first half, Moss would push in the line-outs and in the second he'd jump in the scrums. That would always confuse the English.'

The young players looked up to Moss as if he was God. However, new players from the North found his thick Kerry accent particularly difficult to decipher. The senior players devised a little ritual for those new players. When Trevor Ringland was brought onto the team for the first time they put him beside Moss for dinner, and Trevor was in awe of him. They primed Moss to speak for two minutes in fast forward mode. He was talking pure gibberish. Then he turned to Trevor and asked him what he thought of that. Trevor answered lamely, 'I think you're right,' not having a clue what Moss had said. Then Moss launched off again, only faster. The panic on Trevor's face was a sight to behold. He was going green. All the senior players were killing themselves trying to keep a straight face until Trevor found out he was being wound up.

SWEETS FOR MY SWEET

Folklore about Moss grows with every day and distinguishing fact from fiction is not easy. Moss was playing for the Wolfhounds, and in the side was Charlie Kent, the big blonde English centre. Charlie was a diabetic, and at half-time this rather puffed up ambulance man arrived in the players' huddle and tapped Moss on the shoulder. The man asked Moss if he was the man who wanted a sugar lump. Moss said: 'Arra Jaysus, who do you think I am, Shergar?'

ABSTINENCE

Moss Kean was known to enjoy the occasional drink and, indeed, drink features prominently in the lore of Irish sport. Cork City famously played Bayern Munich in a European tie in 1991. Cork's manager Noel O'Mahony was not too perturbed when asked if he was afraid of losing the away leg, 'We'd still be happy if we lose. It's on the same time as the beer festival.'

Former Irish international Bill 'Wiggs' Mulcahy laughs at the memory of one incident where he got into the spirit of things:

'After one of our trips to Paris I was feeling very, very good at the reception thanks to a large amount of wine. At one stage I went out to the toilet and returned to the top table. I was chatting away in my amazingly dreadful French before I realised that I had got my directions totally wrong and instead of attending the rugby reception, I was at a wedding!'

ODD-SHAPED BALLS

A sport played by women and men with odd-shaped balls is bound to produce great characters and moments of mischief and mirth. Of course, Moss Keane and Willie Duggan are two of the most prominent figures of Irish rugby history.

Hence the story told at a Lions reunion dinner, 'Moss and Willie read that drink was bad for you. They gave up reading.'

THOSE TERRIFIED MEN IN THOSE FLYING MACHINES

Like Willie Duggan, Moss had a fear of flying, and generally the only way they got on a plane was with the benefit of a lot of Dutch courage. As he drove to the airport for the Lions tour in 1977 he was so nervous about the flight that he crashed his car. The story is that he rang his mother just before he took off and said. 'The car is in the airport. It is wrecked. See you in four months.'

THE FEAR FACTOR

Moss was once asked: 'Are you afraid of flying Mossie?'
He replied: 'Afraid of flying? No. Afraid of crashing? Yes.'

A REASONABLE POINT

Moss habitually had to sit on the back seat whenever he took the plane. Asked by Ciaran Fitzgerald why he always took the back seat he replied: 'I've never seen a plane back into a mountain yet.'

MODERATION

Yet a further classic story about Moss goes back to one of his tours with the Barbarians in Wales. At one stage, his team went to the bar after a game of golf. Although everybody else was drinking beer, Moss – with commendable patriotism – was drinking Guinness and was knocking back two pints to everyone else's one. As dinner time approached they decided it was best to return to the team hotel. As people prepared to leave somebody shouted 'One for the road!' Ten pints later for the team at large and twenty pints later for Moss, the team was again summoned to the team bus. Moss was asked if the team should stay for one more drink. He shook his head. When questioned why he was opposed to the idea Moss replied, 'To be sure, I don't want to be making a pig of myself.'

TIGHT TACTICS

Former Irish manager Paul McNaughton recalled a story about Moss for me:
'We were playing against France in 1980 but we lost 19–18. The backs were playing well and we got a bit of confidence, so we decided to run the ball from our own 25. It was unheard of in England, let alone Ireland, to do this at the time. The Irish fans

were completely perplexed at this sudden outpouring of adventure, to see the ball going through hands across the pitch. Then the ball hit Rodney O'Donnell on the shoulder and France got possession and scored a try. All the backs were terrified we'd be dropped for the next match because we'd run the ball. The next time we got a scrum Ollie Campbell asked us which move we wanted to play. As one we all said: "Boot the f**king ball into touch as far up the pitch as possible."

'Roll the clock forward ten years and we were playing in a golden oldies match in Bermuda for Ireland against America. The back line included Mick Quinn, Freddie McLennan, Terry Kennedy and myself. Donal Spring was the captain, but he got sick so Pa Whelan took his place as skipper. When he gave us our tactical talk it was as if we had been caught in a time warp because his tactical instruction was simply: "We're going to keep the ball tight." The backs all looked at each other. I knew the others were thinking the exact same thing as me: "For f**k's sake we're nearly forty. We're playing America. Let's run the f**king ball at last." Moss Keane was our number eight. At the first scrum Pa said: "Okay Mossie, you take the ball on." Mossie made a break, but one of the Americans nearly cut him in half. The Americans had very little skill, but they were ferocious tacklers. At the second scrum Pa said: "Okay Mossie, you take the ball on." Again Mossie made the break and this time one of the Americans nearly killed him with a tackle. The third time we got a scrum Pa said: "Okay let the ball out to the backs." I'll never forget Mick Quinn screeching the immortal words at him: "Hold onto the f**king ball. Ye wanted it. So keep it f**king tight."'

HOW DO YOU LIKE YOUR EGGS IN THE MORNING?

Donal Lenihan was a big admirer of Moss. 'My first full cap against Australia was in 1981 and was really a natural progression from all that went before. Trevor Ringland also made his debut that day. There's always a special friendship between players who won their first caps on the same day. I usually roomed with Moss Keane. He was coming to the end of his career at that stage. Our room was like an alternative medical centre with pollen, garlic tablets and a half-dozen eggs. The mornings of internationals I woke up to see Moss eating three raw eggs. It's not the sort of sight that you want to wake up to.'

Up North

Since his retirement, Mick Quinn has gone on to become known as one of the great raconteurs of Irish rugby. He is so good that it is often hard to distinguish between fact and fiction when he speaks. A month after Moss Keane published his autobiography, Mick met Ollie Campbell and convinced Ollie that the book had sold 70,000 copies in the first month. Even the combined efforts of Roy Keane and Eamon Dunphy couldn't reach those sales figures in a single month. Quinny is also a great mimic and 'does' Moss Keane better than Moss himself. Of Quinn's stories of Moss, the following are my favourites:

'When the troubles in the North were at their height Lansdowne played a match in Belfast. After the match the lads stopped for a case of beer in an off-licence, which would set them up nicely for the train journey home. One evening though there was a bomb scare which ruled out travelling by train, and after a long delay a bus arrived. The problem was that there was no room on the bus for Moss, Rory Moroney and I. Moss had already disposed of a couple of his beers and was not too happy with the prospect of having to wait even longer. He marched onto the bus and said: "Excuse me, this bus is going to crash." At first nobody moved but then a little old man got up and walked up timidly to the towering figure of Moss and said: "Excuse me sir, but where did you say this bus was going to?"'

THE AULD ENEMY

In 1974 Ireland faced England at Twickenham. Although they were underdogs, Ireland won 26–21. Before the game, the Irish players were running onto the pitch when they were stopped in the tunnel by an official in a blazer. He said, 'Tally ho boys. Tally ho. The BBC cameras are not ready for you yet.' The Irish lads were just itching to get on the pitch and found the waiting a pain, particularly when they were joined in the tunnel by the English team. The English were led by their captain, John Pullin, who was shouting at his team about Waterloo. The Irish players couldn't understand what Waterloo had to do with them. The English players looked bigger and stronger than their Irish counterparts. As they were always on television they were all huge stars. The Irish players were studiously trying to avoid eye contact with them, as they planned to rough them up a bit on the pitch. However, Tony Neary went over and tapped Moss on the shoulder and said, 'Moss, best of luck. May the best team win.'

Keane growled back, 'I f**king hope not.'

A MEMORY LAPSE

Moss was interviewed for *The Irish Independent* by the late Sean Diffley in the 1970s. The meeting took place in a hostelry in Rathgar. There was a significant level of liquid refreshment consumed, so much so that Diffo rang Moss the next day to ask: 'What was it that we were talking about yesterday?'

HOME THOUGHTS FROM ABROAD

When Moss went on his first tour to New Zealand with the Lions he was the only player in the first seven weeks who the BBC had not interviewed, because they did not think his strong Kerry brogue would work well with a British audience. Eventually the Lions players said they would refuse to do any more interviews for the BBC until Nigel Starmer-Smith interviewed Moss. Nigel reluctantly agreed to this demand and asked on live television, 'Well Moss, you've been here now for two months and you've played in your first Lions Test, met the Maoris … what's been the best moment of the trip for you?'

In his thickest Kerry accent, Moss replied, 'When I heard that Kerry beat Cork in the Munster final.'

FEELING SHEEPISH

Moss had pulled a hamstring on the plane over and was unable to train for days and days. Eventually the frustrated tour manager went to Phil Bennett, the Lions captain, and said: 'If Moss Keane doesn't train tomorrow, I'm sending him home.' Benny spoke to Moss and the Irish legend agreed to train the following day. It was lashing rain and freezing for the training session and Moss showed up in his shorts, a t-shirt and sneakers. Just before he left the hotel he told the waiter: 'Can you please have some hot coffee and a rasher sandwich ready for me when I come back?' When Moss returned, the waiter handed him a mug of steaming coffee but apologised: 'You won't believe it – we are out of bacon.' Moss looked aghast and stared at him in disbelief: 'Three million sheep in New Zealand – how can you be out of bacon?'

REGULAR HABITS

On that Lions tour in 1977, Moss roomed with Peter Wheeler on the first night. Wheeler was woken up prematurely by Moss turning on his bedside lamp, lighting a cigarette and opening a can of beer. Wheeler exclaimed indignantly: 'It's five o'clock in the morning and we're on a Lions tour to New Zealand.'

Moss answered: 'It's five o'clock in the evening back home in Ireland and I always have a pint at five.'

NO MISTLETOE BUT LOTS OF WINE

For the social aspect, Lions captain Phil Bennett always enjoyed his trips with the Irish contingent. After one post-match dinner some of the Irish players were intent on stretching the evening a bit further and hit a local nightclub. After entering the premises, Moss Keane beckoned to Willie Duggan. 'What'll ye have, Willie?'

Duggan replied, 'Moss, I'll have a creamy pint of stout, from the middle of the barrel.'

After a brief exchange at the bar Moss returned and sad sadly, 'They've no beer here at all, Willie, only wine.'

'Oh,' replied Duggan, 'I'll have a pint of wine, so.'

Later that night Bennett said to Duggan: 'Moss Keane has legs on him like a drinks cabinet.'

Duggan replied: 'That's very appropriate considering the amount he drinks.'

ONE GOOD TURN …

Moss attended a charity auction for GOAL in 1979. He brought the house down when he told how Ireland had lost narrowly to Wales in Cardiff Arms Park earlier in the year, despite a breathtaking performance by Tony Ward. The game is best remembered though for Ireland's full back and future Tánaiste, Dick Spring, dropping a ball, which let Wales in for a soft try and earned Spring the nickname 'Butterfingers' on *Scrap Saturday*. In his own distinctive style, Moss held up a plastic bag and recalled how he had gone into the Welsh dressing room after the game to swap jerseys with Allan Martin, the Welsh forward. On his way out, big Moss remembered that Martin had not been a good man to buy a round of drinks on the Lions tour, so he went back inside and 'borrowed' Martin's tracksuit while he was in the shower, to compensate for all the drinks Keane had bought him on the Lions tour.

COME DINE WITH ME

Similar to Moss, Dick Spring was another distinguished former footballer from Kerry. After a match at Twickenham, Spring and Keane returned home and had a very late night session in St Mary's rugby club. They stayed in Moss' 'high class' flat in Rathmines. They woke up the next day at midday very much the worse for wear and went to Joe's Steakhouse for some food. Moss ordered a mixed grill. Spring's tastes were more modest and he just asked for plaice and chips. When the food arrived Moss looked a bit queasy. He looked up and said, 'Springer, would you ever mind swapping?' Spring duly obliged. That day has entered folklore because it is said to be the only time in his life Moss turned his back on a big meal.

Another time Moss and Spring were together for a match in London. They were both starving on the Saturday night. The two of them crept into the kitchen of their hotel and sought out some food. Suddenly they were caught in the act by the porter. They expected to have the face eaten off them. After a dramatic pause he said, 'You know ye're lucky lads. There's now three Kerry men in the room.' The two lads got the meal of their lives.

BLESSED ARE THE PEACEMAKERS

Moss always said you have to pick your fights. To illustrate, he recalled how he was once selected to play for the Welsh Barbarians against South Africa. The game turned violent, with numerous bouts of fisticuffs. At one stage twenty-nine of the players on the field were fighting ferociously. Moss was the sole non-combatant. Asked later why he was so uncharacteristically Gandhian, Moss replied, 'I might die for Ireland but I'm f**cked if I'm going to die for Wales.'

THE TOWER OF BABEL

Language barriers can be a serious problem in exhibition games. In the 1970s an all-star cast was assembled to play a club team. The celebrity team included Gareth Edwards, Gerald Davies, and the Scot Ian Barnes. Barnes was a second-row forward from the Borders who spoke with a thick Scottish accent. His scrummaging partner was Moss Keane who spoke with a thick Irish accent. Both were sorting out tactics before the match but were incapable of communicating through words. By using gestures and vigorous nods of the head they seemed to have worked something out. The scrum was a total disaster. The touring side were losing by twenty points at half-time. Barnes went to Edwards and said, 'Hey Gareth, I cannae understand what he's saying. I'm pushing on the wrong side of the scrum. Would you think you could get him to swap sides with me?' A minute later Keane went up to Edwards and said, 'That bloody Scot can't speak f**king English. I'm pushing on the wrong side.' Edwards brokered a compromise and the tourists were a transformed side in the second half and won the match.

MR NICE

Moss was renowned for his consideration for others. One night before a home international the Irish team were staying in the Shelbourne Hotel. In the middle of the night, he decided to go into Mike Kiernan and Paul Dean's room and use their bathroom rather than use the one he shared with Willie Duggan. Puzzled as to why he chose to use their toilet Dean asked Moss what he was doing. Big Moss replied: 'Willie doesn't like me using our toilet when he is in the room.'

CROWNING GLORY

In 1982 before the Triple Crown decider against Scotland, Bill Beaumont rang Keane to wish him well. 'Moss. If you win they will build a statue of you in Cork.'

'Billy, you bo***x. I'm a Kerryman.'

Moss had some moments of confusion himself. After the game was over Moss approached Ciaran Fitzgerald and said, 'I'm taking the Cup to Currow next weekend. No more about it – my mind is made up.'

'But Moss, there is no trophy. The Triple Crown is a mythical trophy.'

'Is there a medal?' Moss asked.

'No, Moss.'

'You mean to say we went to all that f**king trouble and they won't even give us a f**king medal?'

BESTSELLER

Moss had his autobiography ghostwritten by Billy Keane. Shortly after, he ran into Peter Clohessy. The Claw politely remarked: 'I see you got Billy Keane to write a book for you, Moss.'

Moss replied: 'You did? Who read it to you?'

BON VOYAGE

When Ireland toured Australia in 1979 Moss came to the attention of the immigration desk at Sydney. Nobody was sure what started off the heated argument between Moss and one of the officials, which culminated in the official asking sharply: 'Do you have any previous convictions.'

Moss replied disdainfully: 'I didn't know you still needed a conviction to enter Australia.'

A MATTER OF PRINCIPLE

Old rugby players never die – they simply have their balls taken away.

Even after his retirement Jim Glennon, to his own surprise, continued to grace the world's playing fields. When he finished playing in 1988 he got the most unexpected invitations to tour as the 'Golden Oldies' idea was really taking off. He got a phone call from Moss Keane in June of that year enquiring if he was free for the last weekend in August. When Jim said he was, Moss told him to keep it free. Jim forgot all about it until the last Wednesday in August when he got another call from Moss. Moss told him that he had been invited to play in an exhibition match across the water for a Lions' Golden Oldies side against a junior team, and although he had been given the plane ticket he was unable to travel. He was going to ring the organiser and tell him he couldn't make it, but that he would be meeting Jim later that day and would attempt to persuade him to travel. Shortly afterwards Glennon got a phone call from a panic-stricken secretary, apologising profusely for the short notice, but wondering would he be willing to play instead of Moss. Jim 'reluctantly' agreed.

On the plane over he was joined by Phil Orr, Willie Duggan and Fergus Slattery. It was a fabulous weekend. Glennon was the only 'non-Lion' on the team. His partner in the second row was Allan Martin of Wales. After the match the pair were chatting in the bath when Martin asked him out of the blue, 'What about Stockholm?' He went on to explain that there was a Golden Oldies match there the following week, Thursday to Monday, but he couldn't travel. 'Would you be interested?' When Glennon said yes Allan told Jim just to leave it with him. On the Monday Jim rang Moss to thank him for the wonderful weekend, and asked him why he had left it so late to tell them he couldn't make it. Moss answered, 'Because I didn't want some hoor from England to take my place.'

Two days later, Jim got a phone call from a different panic-stricken secretary, apologising profusely for the short notice, but wondering would he be willing to play instead of Allan. This time Jim made him sweat a bit more and told him he wasn't sure if he would be able to make it because he had other commitments, but he rang him back less than an hour later and agreed to the trip. On the plane over he was again joined by Orr, Duggan and Slattery. Also on the trip were J. P. R. Williams and Jim Renwick, amongst others. It was an absolutely fabulous weekend. On the Tuesday morning Jim rang to thank Allan for putting it his way. When he asked him why he had left it so late to tell them he couldn't make it, he replied, 'Because I didn't want some hoor from England to take my place!'

A FINAL MESSAGE

Almost until his last breath Moss retained a deep love of Munster rugby. Hours before he died he was visited by his old friend from Lansdowne, Mick Quinn, who had the privilege of spending ten minutes on his own with one of the most loved figures in Irish sport. Moss was very ill at the time, but as Quinny was leaving he promised him he would drive down to Portarlington to see him again the following day. Moss beckoned him closer, and with a waving finger said: 'Ye bast**ds from Leinster beat us again last Saturday.'

My favourite Moss story though comes not from Mick Quinn, but from the late, much missed Dermot Morgan, long before his role in *Father Ted*. Dermot told the story of Moss strolling purposefully into the pub one night and on seeing all his mates said to them: 'Would you mind if I stayed on my own tonight, I've only enough money for eight pints!'

CHAPTER THREE

Munster Magic

It was Mae West who famously observed, 'A hard man is good to find.' In Irish rugby we found one in Peter Clohessy. He knew how to mix it. He believed that a good prop forward should be so mean that if he owned the Atlantic Ocean he wouldn't give you a wave. The Claw is one of the many Munster legends, and this chapter pays tribute to them.

PAINTING BY NUMBERS

Clohessy earned the nickname 'Judge Dredd' in the dressing room because his word was law. It was evident from an early age that the Claw was going to be the strong silent type. According to folklore when he was four he went to the dentist, who tried to strike up a conversation with the future rugby legend. 'How old are you?'

No response.

'Don't you know how old you are?'

Immediately four fingers went up. 'Okay', the dentist then asked, 'and do you know how old that is?'

Four little fingers went up once again. Continuing the effort to get a response the dentist asked, 'Can you talk?'

The young Clohessy looked at him menacingly and asked, 'Can you count?'

Down to earth

Clohessy is said to be the only man in Limerick who can leave his car unlocked. As the Claw once told me though, he could be the focus of strong criticism even in his home city:

'One Tuesday evening after a particularly galling loss to Shannon I was heading onto the field to go training for Young Munster and there was this old lady, I'd say she was eighty-five if she was a day, and she called me over to the wire. I knew I was in for an earful straight away. She shouted at me: "What the hell was wrong with you on Saturday? You were hoisted so high in the scrum I was going to send you a parachute."'

Priorities

The home of Limerick rugby, Thomond Park, is famous for the twenty foot wall which envelops it but which is unable to prevent the ball from leaving the grounds from time to time. When balls were lost, the crowd were wont to shout: 'Never mind the ball, get on with the game!'

Sir, yes sir!

Clohessy's keen brain was to the fore in one of the bonding exercises before the Lions tour in 1997. As is common practice with rugby teams, they were taken to a military base for exercises. At one point they were given an instruction in unarmed self-defence. After their instructor presented a number of different situations in which they might find themselves, he asked Clohessy, 'What steps would you take if someone were coming at you with a large, sharp knife?'

The Claw replied, 'Big ones.'

BADLY BURNT

Before the 2002 Heineken Cup semi-final the Claw faced a serious injury when he was badly burnt in a domestic accident. This prompted his wife to remark: 'I always felt you'd go out in a blaze of glory but I didn't think you'd literally do it.' The small matter of multiple skin burns was not enough to deter Clohessy from playing in the game. In solidarity with the Claw, Munster fans wore t-shirts to the game saying: 'Bitten and burnt, but not beaten.'

THE GOSPEL ACCORDING TO LUKE

One of the stories that illustrates the Claw's passion for the game goes back to the first time he saw his son Luke play a game, and Clohessy senior was voicing strong opinions from the sidelines about the referee. After one of the Claw's many vocal contributions, the coach called Luke over to the sideline and said to him, 'Do you understand what cooperation is? What team is?'

Luke nodded in the affirmative.

'Do you understand that what matters is whether we win together as a team?'

The little boy nodded yes.

'So,' the coach continued, 'when a penalty is awarded you don't argue or curse or attack the ref. Do you understand all that?'

Again Luke nodded.

'Good,' said the coach, 'now go over there and explain it to your father.'

MERCY KILLING

The classic Clohessy story, which I stress is apocryphal, involves the referee who decides that he has to make a quick getaway after an Irish international against England in Lansdowne Road, in which he sent off three Irish players and awarded two controversial penalties. He drives too quickly, crashes coming round a bend and is thrown through the windscreen onto the road. By coincidence, the car following him is driven by one of the players he sent off, Peter Clohessy, and he stops to see if he can help. He finds that the referee is in a bad way and makes a 999 call on his mobile.

'I think the referee's dead,' he shouts down the phone in panic. 'What can I do?'

'Calm down,' says the operator, used to dealing with emergencies. 'First of all, go and make sure the referee is dead.'

The operator hears a choking sound and the cracking of neck bone. Then the Claw returns to the mobile.

'Okay,' he says. 'I've made sure he's dead. Now what should I do?'

SWEET MEMORIES

The Claw looks back on his career with affection:

'What I remember most is all the good times we had on and off the pitch. Although we trained hard, we had a lot of fun. My fondest memory is before we played Scotland one time. The night before the match Mick Galwey discovered his togs were missing. There was a minor panic because nobody else had any to spare. Eventually someone got him togs. Ireland were sponsored by Nike at the time. The problem was Mick's togs didn't have the Nike name or swish, so someone gave him a black marker and he wrote the name Nike on the togs. Later that night I crept in to his room and changed the word 'Nike' to 'Mike' and wrote 'Mike loves Joan'. The next day we were changing in the dressing room before the match when I saw Mick putting on his togs. He didn't notice the change but noticed I was laughing at him. He asked: "Okay, what have you done to me?" When I told him he had a great laugh. It was just an hour before a big international but it was a great way of breaking the ice for us.'

MY WAY

In conversation with this writer, Ronan O'Gara observed: 'I suppose the two greatest characters in my time were Mick Galwey and Peter Clohessy. They were old school … the freshness they brought to the game and to the Irish squad was very uplifting. Probably my abiding memory of my days in the Irish squad was when the players and management made a presentation to Peter to mark his fiftieth cap. Peter responded by singing the Frank Sinatra song, 'I did it my way'. What an appropriate song. He did things his way or no way. That's why I liked him and admired him so much.'

GUMP

Donncha O'Callaghan is the clown prince of Irish rugby. Yet he has a serious side and a big heart, as is evident in his charity work for UNICEF and his mercy mission to Haiti after their earthquake in 2010.

A case in point was after Rob Henderson required fifteen stitches in his lip following a 'clash' in a Celtic League match in autumn 2004. Noticing Hendo's concern about his appearance, his ever helpful teammate O'Callaghan called him 'Bubba' after the character in Forrest Gump.

TOUCH WOOD

Tony O'Reilly tells a great story about Brendan Behan. Behan turned up to a chat show on Canadian television totally drunk. The presenter was very unimpressed and asked him why he was so drunk. Behan replied, 'Well a few weeks ago I was sitting in a pub in Dublin and I saw a sign on a beer mat which said: "Drink Canada Dry." So when I came over here I said I'd give it a go.' O'Reilly deftly uses that incident to speak of the need to have the kind of positive attitude that says, 'I'll give it a go.'

FAIL TO PREPARE ...

That was the kind of upbeat mentality Keith Gerard Mallinson Wood played with.

Wood was a stickler for preparing properly though. This sometimes brought problems in the run-up to his marriage. His wife-to-be was telling him about her dreams for their wedding. Keith, on the other hand, had has his mind on one of Ireland's upcoming internationals and was not listening properly. His fiancée noticed this and decided to test him on how much he had taken in: 'So, what's my favourite flower?

Woodie thought deeply: 'Self-raising.'

UNCLE FESTER

From the outset Woodie was recognised as not just one of the great rugby players, but also one of the great characters in world rugby. His irreverent wit endeared himself to everyone.

The bald wonder first captained Ireland against Australia in November 1996 and immediately established himself as an inspirational leader. His motivational qualities were very evident in one of the most tangible legacies of the 1997 Lions Tour when England's John 'Bentos' Bentley made as big a name for himself off the pitch as he did on it with his critically acclaimed video account of the trip; *Living with Lions* set the bar for all subsequent fly-on-the-wall sporting documentaries.

One of the most striking parts of the video were Woodie's passionate outbursts before games. It was as though his tactic was to try and equalise before the other side scored. However, Woodie's one blemish was also to emerge on the trip. Bentley had the misfortune to be rooming with him. As a result of his shoulder problems Keith could only sleep in one position. He propped two pillows under both shoulders and as soon as he began to sleep he started snoring loudly. After seven sleepless nights, Bentley could take no more and sought medical advice. On the eighth night, as soon as Woodie started sleeping, Bentley kissed him on the cheek. For the next three nights Woodie lay awake in case Bentley made further advances on him.

SLEEPING WITHOUT BEAUTY

Tom Smith, the Scottish prop and star of the 1997 Lions tour, was known as 'the silent assassin' because he was so quiet. However, one night on that tour he was sleepwalking, and his roommate Mark 'Ronnie' Regan woke up to find Smith coming towards him with his hands out as he was ready to choke him. Henceforth Smith was rechristened 'the Boston Strangler'.

HAIR-RAISING

Keith Wood wreaked havoc on that tour – mostly on Matt Dawson's hair. Finding himself rooming with Fester, Dawson decided the baldest man on the tour was the best man to give him a haircut. Woody was more interested in recalling a story about a man from Cork with a one-eyed dog who walked into a lamppost, so he was not really paying attention and left Dawson with what the scrum half described as 'a reverse Mohican', having cut a swathe out of the middle of his hair. Dawson realised something was seriously wrong when the unthinkable happened – Wood went completely quiet. Woodie had shaved off all his hair.

BROTHERS IN ARMS

In 1997, before the Lions went on tour to World Champions South Africa a Cape Town reporter carried the headline: 'These are not Lions but pussycats.' The Lions had the last laugh, as they won the series.

Key to the success of the tour was the unity of purpose shared by all in the party, players and management, a unity that was missing four years later. The players did some unusual things to keep spirits up.

New nicknames were lavishly doled out. Lawrence Dallaglio was nicknamed 'Lawrence Bowlegglio', because you could drive a bus through his legs. Jeremy Davidson's nickname became 'Buzz Lightyear' because of his jaw, which always looked like he was chewing marbles. Will Greenwood was nicknamed 'Shaggy' because he looks like the character from *Scooby Doo*. Keith Wood became 'The Irish Sperm Whale'.

The Lions kept tabs to ensure that miscreants were punished appropriately for their misdemeanours, such as poor dress sense. For his transgressions Austin Healey, 'The Gimp', was stripped to his underpants and an apple was stuck in his mouth and tied to his head with electrical tape, in a recreation of the scene from *Pulp Fiction*.

When a friend rang from England, Will Greenwood took the call and said: 'Austin can't come to the phone. He's a bit tied up at the moment.'

While he was bound Healey asked if he could go to the toilet. 'Only if you recite the alphabet,' replied Lawrence Dallaglio. 'Okay,' said Austin. 'ABCDEFGHIJKLMNOQRSTUVWXYZ.'

'Where's the P?' asked Dallaglio.

'Halfway down my leg,' said Healey.

IN YOUR FACE

Woodie's style of captaincy was in-your-face. Matt Dawson recalls playing against Mpumalanga on the Lions tour in 1997, when Wood was captain for a midweek game. He went to Dawson in the dressing room and pressed his forehead on his. Then he started shaking him around, not butting him but pushing his forehead into him, sweating all over him, shouting at him, spitting in his face. Although Dawson confesses it 'scared the crap' out of him, he went on to play a great game and the Lions won 64–14.

GREEN FINGERS

English winger Dan Luger tells the story about the man who loved his garden in the days when Woodie was an amateur. One day his world almost ended when he woke up to see that his pride and joy was scarred by a proliferation of molehills. He was distraught. He soon wiped his tears, got out the *Yellow Pages* and saw an ad which read: 'For the best mole catcher in town, call Keith Wood – simply the best.'

Woodie was on the job instantly. He promised the man he would solve the problem. He stood on watch all night hoping to catch the mole but with no luck. The next night he repeated the vigil but again with no sign of the mole. By now the garden owner was irate and said to Wood, 'When you catch this damned mole, make him die the worst death you can imagine – really nasty.'

The next morning Wood was jubilant, 'I caught him, just as I promised.'

'That's wonderful news. How did you kill him?'

'Horribly,' replied Woodie, 'I buried him alive.'

FORLORN IN THE USA

According to legend, Woodie went to Dallas after the 2003 World Cup for a well deserved vacation. He checked into a downtown hotel, but when he got to his room he immediately called the front desk. Keith said, 'This here bed can sleep the whole Munster team. I only wanted a regular sized bed.'

The clerk responded, 'That is a regular sized bed, sir. You have to remember that everything's big in Texas.'

Woodie went to the hotel's bar and ordered a draught beer. When he was served, he said to the bartender, 'This is as big as Peter Clohessy. I only asked for a glass of beer.'

The bartender answered, 'That is a glass of beer, sir. You have to remember that everything's big in Texas.'

When the waiter in the hotel's dining room brought out the

steak Keith ordered for dinner, Woodie exclaimed, 'That steak's as big as John Hayes' thigh and the baked potato is bigger than Reggie Corrigan's head. Where'd this come from?'

The waiter replied, 'It's all local, sir. You have to remember that everything's big in Texas.'

When the waiter asked Woodie if he wanted to see the dessert menu, Keith said he might be able to squeeze something in, but after consuming all that food and drink he needed to use the restroom first. The waiter directed him to go down the hall to the first door on the right.

By this time, Wood was quite inebriated and mistakenly went through the first door on the left. He walked across the tiled floor and fell into the swimming pool.

When the rugby legend came spluttering to the surface, he yelled out, 'For f**k's sake, please don't flush.'

LUCKY STREAK

Another story told about Woodie goes back to the 2001 Lions tour. Graham Henry was surprised to see Wood hanging up a horseshoe on the wall. Henry said with a nervous laugh, 'Surely you don't believe that horseshoe will bring you good luck, do you, Keith?'

Wood chuckled, 'I believe no such thing, coach. Not at all. I am scarcely likely to believe in such foolish nonsense. However, I am told that a horseshoe will bring you good luck whether you believe in it or not.'

HOOKERS

Murray Mexted was the All Blacks number eight for nine years. Like George Best, he has an interesting personal life. He married Miss Universe. The conventional wisdom is: those who can do, those who can't talk about it. Mexted is the exception to the rule.

Since his retirement from the game he has become one of the best known rugby commentators down under, though more for his idiosyncratic use of language than for his insights into the game. He described a helicopter drying a ground in New Zealand as: 'It's just like a giant blow job.' His analysis of a ball kicked on a wet ground was: 'My father used to call it a testicles kick because you actually ended with your balls up.' His most famous comment about an Irish player concerned Keith Wood tackling like a man possessed. 'You don't like to see hookers going down on players like that.'

THE LYONS DEN

In Kerry, you are considered to have an inferiority complex if you only consider yourself to be as good as everybody else, so it comes as little surprise to discover that Kerrymen like Mick Galwey, who played for Ireland, did not lack in confidence.

History casts a long shadow in the area in Kerry where Galwey grew up. Memories of the Irish Civil War lasted a very long time. This was most tellingly revealed in a conversation between a De Valera fan and a Michael Collins fan in the 1960s.

The Dev fan said: 'De Valera was as straight as Christ and as spiritually strong.'

The Collins fan replied: 'Wasn't it a great pity the hoor wasn't crucified as young.'

In a previous life Galwey played senior football for Kerry. The high point of his career with the Kingdom was when he came on as a sub in the All-Ireland semi-final against Meath in 1986. It was a bruising encounter, as he found himself marking one of the hardest men in the history of the game – Mick Lyons.

The encounter with Lyons was the second biggest fright of Galwey's life. According to legend, the biggest came one night in his courting days when he took a shortcut through a graveyard and he heard a tapping sound. As he walked, the tapping got louder and his fright grew into terror. Suddenly, he came across a man crouched down, chiselling at a gravestone.

'Oh, thank goodness,' Gaillimh said with great relief. 'You frightened me. I didn't know what that noise was. What are you doing?'

The other man turned his face into the moonlight as he said to the rugby star, 'They spelt my name wrong.'

Local strife

'Gaillimh' loves the rivalry between Cork and Limerick rugby. Some have said that in Munster rugby Cork is the political wing, Limerick the military.

Putting the boot in

Mick Quinn tells a story about Galwey and Will Carling. The famous English captain was not loved universally by his teammates. When Ireland played England it was a typically robust match. After a heated ruck, where boots were flying with more frequency than planes at an airport, everyone picked themselves off the muddy pitch to reveal the man at the bottom of the pile of bodies. It was Carling. He had a huge gash under his eye. The referee, slightly shocked that the English captain should be the victim of such thuggery, asked: 'Right, own up, who did this?'

Immediately Galwey piped up, 'Take your pick ref, it could have been any one of the twenty-nine of us.'

The apprentice

Mick is one of rugby's great diplomats. He is loathe to criticise anybody. Like many Kerry people, you have to read between the lines to figure out what he is saying. When asked his opinion about Brian Ashton's tenure as Irish coach, he kicks for touch. Galwey denies that towards the ignominious end of Ashton's reign one of the Irish squad said to him: 'Tell me, how long have you been with us, not counting tomorrow?'

It was rumoured that a prominent Irish official said to Ashton: 'Today I'm going to mix business and pleasure. You're fired.'

YOUNG AT HEART

Gaillimh retains fond memories of his time with Ireland: 'Woodie was one player who could turn a game. He played hurling and Gaelic football in Clare, and that didn't do him any harm. Woodie was the world's number one hooker but he was still one of the lads. He was one of the Limerick under-14s, as we called them, with myself and Peter Clohessy. Of course, Clohessy is one of the great characters of Irish sport. I remember once playing in France with Munster when Peter got a bad knock in the knee and had to be carried off. It was the strangest sight I ever saw in a match because the guys who brought on the stretcher for him were wearing wellingtons. I said to the Claw, "Don't worry. The fire brigade are coming."'

THE BARE FACTS

A later addition to that trio was Rob Henderson. My first meeting with Henderson was memorable. On the eve of a Munster–Leinster Celtic League match Rob invited me up to his hotel room. When I knocked at the door he ushered me in. I was more than a little taken aback to discover that all he was 'wearing' was a bath towel. Despite many hours of expensive therapy I have never been able to erase that very disturbing image from the dark corners of my subconscious.

So this is Christmas

During his playing days with London Irish Henderson came under the stewardship of Clive Woodward. Apart from getting to know him as a coach, they also got to know each other socially:

'I've spent some time with him. I've even had Christmas dinner with him. I invited myself. We had a delightful Christmas. He's a lovely fella and he's very smart. He was as good at business as he was at organising the England team. The guy is focused to the nth degree. I expected that he would do a great job coaching the Lions. I told that to everyone I could think of who knew him before the tour in the hope he might pick me. He got the results he did with England because he got the best out of people. He did that by giving everything he had to give; he doesn't do anything unless he does it wholeheartedly.

'I played golf with him one day. I'd started playing two or three months beforehand but I'd got all the gear from a sponsor. We came to the first tee and I hit one down the middle, which was a miracle. I was really keyed up but by the time I got to the eighth hole I had lost all the balls in my bag and about fourteen of Clive's. He loves his golf, and when I hit another ball into the woods he just looked at me sadly and said: "I think we better go in now."

'I gave him the green jersey I wore when I won my first cap for Ireland. I presented it in a grand manner as befits Clive – in a Tesco bag. He wasn't there when I dropped it into his home, so he wrote to me and said when I eventually grew up he would return it to me.'

The Wizard of Oz

The late Cliff Morgan described touring with the Lions as 'breaking bread with the rest of the world'. The high point of Henderson's career was the Lions tour of Australia in 2001. To make the trip in the first place was fantastic, but to play in all of the three Tests was wonderful. Hendo's awesome power was the perfect foil for Brian O'Driscoll's sublime skills and they provided the coach, Graham Henry, with the perfect midfield combination of strength and flair. Henderson's teammates were not so appreciative of his off the field activities. Rooming with Henderson was the ultimate nightmare, according to Austin Healey, because he smokes like a chimney and snores liked a blocked up chimney.

RALA

Rob Henderson loves the big personalities in Irish rugby:

'A real character is Patrick O'Reilly. He played hooker for Terenure and is now the kitman for the Irish team. Everybody knows him as "Rala". He got the nickname because when he was in Irish class at school he was brought up to the blackboard and told to write his name. After he wrote Rala he couldn't remember the Irish version of the rest of his surname so all the kids called him Rala and the name stuck for the rest of his life. If you ever need advice, shoelaces, or you were ever in a scrape or you needed help he's the "go-to man", as they would say in the NFL. If he can't do it he will find someone who can. The only problem is that he delegates his work to everybody else. He may have fifteen bags but he'll have sixteen people who want to help him carry them. He's a guy who I will never forget.

'He tells a great story of playing against Garryowen when his opposite number was the former Irish hooker, and later manager, Pa Whelan. It was a windy day with a howling gale. A call came in from the second row but Rala couldn't hear it. One of the second rows stepped forward and said to Rala: "Low and hard at number two." Rala shrugged his shoulders and stepped back. He then threw the ball very hard at Pa Whelan. Rala spent the next forty-five minutes both apologising and running away from him.'

ANGIE

Henderson's most loyal fan was his wife, Angie, who offers a revealing insight into the legendary status of one player in the Irish set-up:

'Peter Clohessy left more than just a hole in Irish rugby when he retired in 2002 – he left his seat at the back of the bus vacant too. I was amused to find, like a school bus, the team coach had the naughty, big boys who always sat on the back seat. The "usual suspects" included the Claw, Woodie, Axel Foley and Rob. In 2003 after joining the team on their coach to travel the short journey across town for a celebratory dinner, I found a spare seat that just happened to be next to the man I married. The conversation unfolded as follows:

Me: "Oh that's nice, darling, you saved me a seat …"
Rob: "That's Claw's seat …"
Me: "But Rob, Claw's not here, he didn't play; he's retired."
Rob: "Yeah … but it's still his seat."'

HENDO

Some sports personalities are in the business of self-denial. When the former Chelsea player, Adrian Mutu, was asked why he tested positive for cocaine he replied: 'I got into this situation because of some complicated matters with my soul.' Hendo is refreshingly candid. He has his fair share of rugby stories, but his favourites deal with the exploits of one former Irish international:

'My favourite character is Ken O'Connell, the former Irish international. His nickname is "the Legend" but you would have to know him to understand why. He gained his legendary status in a different way to Brian O'Driscoll. He went off to India or Thailand to find himself. We played together with London Irish. At one stage we were playing in the European Conference. We were all there getting ready to travel to Bordeaux. We were getting kitted out and were all there with our kitbags as if we were heading to Monaco. We looked a million dollars. Just as we were ready to leave someone shouted: "Where's Ken?" Half an hour later he shows up with Malcolm O'Kelly. For once, miraculously, Mal had all his gear and luggage. Somebody must have dressed him. Ken turned up wearing a t-shirt and shorts. His t-shirt had a picture of a fella wearing shorts and a t-shirt, but with his "manhood" sticking out. His only luggage was a kitbag which was the size of a big ice cream tub. I said: "Ken, what are you carrying mate?"

'He replied: "I've got all I need. I've got my boots, my gumshield and my heart." With that he was off to get the plane. That's Ken boy. That's why he's a legend.

'I will never forget my first introduction to Ken. Before he played his first game for London Irish, he wandered into the changing room with his togs around his ankles. He looked down at his private parts and said to me: "I bet you thought Saint Patrick chased all the snakes out of Ireland."'

THANK YOU FOR THE MUSIC

Rob is also a talented songwriter. The 2001 Lions tour to Australia was a very unhappy one, particularly for the Lions players who did not play in the Test series. Rob rewrote the Travis hit *Driftwood*, which became their mantra:

> *Australia's an island*
> *A long long way from home*
> *We're touring with the Lions*
> *And feeling all alone*
>
> *Big games at the weekend*
> *With nothing in between*
> *Except training until sunset*
> *Trying to look keen*

Do you know what I mean!
We're driftwood
Touring with the Lions
Playing on a Tuesday, Tuesday, Tuesday …

Backhander

'The hand of God and the hand of Diego.' This was the explanation Diego Maradona of Argentina gave after he deflected the ball with his hand over the advancing England goalkeeper, Peter Shilton, in the 1986 World Cup. His goal helped Argentina to victory and they went on to take the World Cup. To this day, it is one of the most famous incidents of ethical dimensions in world sport.

The most talked about 'ethical incident' in rugby occurred in the final moments of the Heineken Cup final in 2002. Munster were trailing Leicester and were driving hard for their opponents' line when they were awarded a set scrum some five metres out from goal. It was crucial to win this ball and set up a final drive for possible victory. As Peter Stringer was about to put the ball into the scrum, Neil Back's infamous 'hand of God' backhander, knocked the ball from the Munster scrum half's grasp into the Leicester scrum and the ball was lost to Leicester. The referee had taken up a position opposite the incoming ball and did not see the incident.

The controversy spawned a new joke:

Q: What's the difference between Tim Henman and Neil Back?

A: Neil Back is much better with his backhand.

Cheating

The manner of the defeat in the 2002 Heineken Cup final, Neil Back's infamous 'backhander', left a bitter taste. One Munster fan was heard to remark: 'The Leicester Tigers should be renamed the Leicester Cheetahs.'

They also told the story about Back himself. In this account, Back went on a ski trip but was knocked unconscious by the chairlift. He called his insurance company from the hospital, but it refused to cover his injury.

'Why is this injury not covered?' he asked.

'You got hit in the head by a chairlift,' the insurance rep said. 'That makes you an idiot, and we consider that a pre-existing condition.'

MURDER MOST FOUL

In 2001 Harlequins travelled to play Munster in the Heineken Cup. As it was a crunch match and Munster were very difficult to beat at home, the Quins players went to bed early. Two of Quins' English internationals Will Greenwood – aka Rodney Trotter, according to some English fans – and Tony 'Dippers' Diprose were rooming together. Very early in the morning they were rudely awoken by a loud banging on the door. They assumed it was someone straggling in from a nightclub who didn't know where he was and didn't respond. But the banging continued. Then a booming voice said: 'This is the police, open up.'

The two internationals replied in unison: 'Yeh, yeh, sure, p*** off, will you.'

'Open up immediately, there has been a murder,' said the booming voice.

'Very funny, now p*** off.' They were convinced it was a wind-up. As the banging persisted, and the tone in the man's voice became more imperative, Dippers eventually got up and opened the door, where he was confronted by two massive policemen. 'About time too,' said one. 'There has been a murder, we would like to question you.'

The rugby stars were immediately freaked out – worrying that one of their teammates might have been killed. The talkative policeman walked into the room and immediately recognised

Greenwood, the centre with a phenomenal try strike rate, who had twice toured with the Lions: 'Oh, hello Will, howya doing?' The fact that he was in the middle of a murder hunt was forgotten. For his part, Greenwood was bursting to know the details of the crime and have his anxieties about his teammates placated, but the policeman continued: 'Nice to welcome you to Munster, I'm sure there'll be a warm reception for you at Thomond Park this afternoon. Anyway, the weather is due to be blustery, may be a hint of rain, wasn't it a great result for the Irish, beating you recently?' The two English players were subjected to the policeman's views on every aspect of the game for almost half an hour, but no reference to the murder. The two players were anxious to get the details and then get back to sleep and eventually managed to steer the police man to the murder. He replied: 'Oh yes, that murder, it obviously wasn't you two, we know that, but lovely to chat. Oh and by the way, Munster will win today.'

He was right.

DONAL'S GEMS

Put-downs were a particular speciality of Donal Lenihan. During the 1989 Lions tour of Australia Lenihan's ready wit was to the fore on a number of occasions. At one stage Bridgend's Mike Griffiths asked, 'Can I ask a stupid question?'

'Better than anyone I know,' answered Lenihan.

Another time the touring party were driving through Sydney when they passed a couple coming out of a church after being married. In all earnestness Jeremy Guscott asked: 'Why do people throw rice at weddings?' Lenihan replied immediately: 'Because rocks hurt.' He then turned defence into attack, 'Why do you think they are getting married, Jeremy?'

'I suppose, Donal, it's because they love each other.'

'I wanted a reason, and you gave me an excuse.'

Jeremy replied, 'Don't be so cynical. Marriage is a great institution.'

Donal nodded his head in agreement, 'Marriage is a great institution all right. It's holy deadlock.'

Scott Hastings grew impatient when his brother Gavin seemed to prefer playing tennis or going windsurfing with Ieuan Evans rather than with him. Lenihan commented: 'Ieuan's like the brother Gavin never had.'

'What about me?' asked Scott.

'You're the brother he did have,' responded Lenihan.

After defeating Australian Capital Territories 27–11 in 1989 Lenihan brought the touring Lions party to the Friends of Ireland bar where they were greeted by a priest. After much liquid refreshment it was time for the team to return to their hotel. The priest bade them farewell. Slightly under the influence one of the 'star players' Andy Robinson told the minister he was wearing his collar back to front.

'I'm a father, Andrew,' said the priest.

'I've got kids myself,' replied Robinson.

'No, I'm the father to hundreds of people in this area,' explained the priest.

'Really. In that case, it's not your collar you should be wearing back to front, it's your bloody trousers.'

Rob Andrew was the only one to put one over on Lenihan on the tour. On a night off he invited Donal to *La Traviata*. Thinking they were going to a nice Italian restaurant Lenihan agreed. What he failed to realise was that they'd been given complimentary tickets to the opera.

EBONY AND IVORY

Towards the end of January 1981, forty-four Irish rugby players received a letter from the IRFU requesting that they indicate if they were available for the Irish short tour of South Africa in May–

June. The letters went out amidst a welter of controversy as political, clerical and media people objected to the notion of Ireland having sporting contact with South Africa, due to the apartheid system which existed there. A number of players declined the invitation. Perhaps the bravest decision not to travel of all was that of Hugo MacNeill, who was just establishing his international place at the time. It took remarkable moral courage for an emerging star to turn down his first overseas tour with his country.

Hugo did manage to extract some fun out of the touring situation though. Around about this time there was a lot of money being offered under the table for players to play in exhibition games in South Africa. One of the ways Hugo sometimes wound up his colleagues in the Irish team was to ring them up, put on a South African accent and offer them £25,000 to play in such a match. It was always interesting to see who showed great interest.

When Donal Lenihan was captain of Ireland and Munster Hugo rang him and pretended to be a chap called Fritz Voller from the South African Rugby Board. He said: 'I'm ringing you in connection with the permission we got from the IRFU to allow you to play in a special match we've arranged between the Springboks and a world selection. The match will be played on October 14.'

Donal replied: 'I'm sorry. I'm totally committed to my responsibilities with Munster and Ireland and I'm unable to make the trip, but thank you for the kind invitation.'

'But we would like you to captain our world selection.'

'I'm sorry, I can't make it because of my commitments to Munster and Ireland.'

'But you could have a nice holiday, and your wife could come with you and stay on for an extended holiday when you return to Ireland.'

'No. I can't because of my commitments to Munster and Ireland.'

'Okay I hear what you're saying. I don't want to put you under undue pressure. Thanks for listening. I suppose there's no point in saying that your match fee would be £30,000.'

There was a pregnant pause.

'Sorry?'

'Oh, I was just mentioning your match fee would be £30,000. It would be lodged into a Swiss bank account. But I wouldn't want to compromise your commitment to Munster and Ireland.'

'That's okay. Sorry, what date in October did you say again? Let me recheck my diary. Now that I think of it my poor wife, Mary, needs a little holiday.'

At which point Hugo rapidly reverted to his own accent and said: 'Lenihan, I've got you by the balls.'

Them and us

Lenihan was also left musing on the historical unfairness of Ireland's relationship with Australia: 'We gave them thousands of our emigrants, which helped to make their county great. What did they give us in return? *Neighbours* and *Home and Away*.'

Injuries forced Lenihan to depart from the international stage slightly ahead of schedule, having captained Ireland seventeen times. 'I knew it was time to retire when the bits and pieces started falling off my body.'

He cut his teeth as Ireland team manager, but resigned to concentrate on his job with the Lions. The former England rugby coach Jack Rowell was once asked what it was like to be a top rugby coach. He replied, 'You have fifteen players in a team. Seven hate your guts and the other eight are making up their minds.' Lenihan was to find out what he meant.

His stewardship of the Lions in 2001 was made more difficult by damning claims about the squad's preparation and training methods made by two Lions players, Matt Dawson and Austin Healey, in articles during the tour. That controversy, and the fact that the Lions lost the series, did take away some of the shine of what should have been the crowning glory of Lenihan's career. It was a case of what might have been. A friend of Donal's put the scale of the disappointment well: 'It was like thinking you have gone to bed with Liz Hurley only to wake up to the terrible realisation that you slept with Red Hurley.'

THE FRENCH CONNECTION

In 1982, having already secured the Triple Crown, Ireland travelled to France hoping to win the Grand Slam. The Irish team bus entered the stadium and was surrounded by French supporters who were going crazy, thumping the side of the bus and shouting abuse at the team. The Irish team was very tense and everyone was silent. Donal Lenihan was sitting beside Moss Finn. The French fans were screaming: *'L'Irelande est fini. L'Irelande est fini'* – 'Ireland is finished.'

Moss Finn stood up and said, 'Christ, lads. Isn't it great to be recognised.'

WORDSMITH

Finn's teammate Michael Kiernan is a master of the put-down. Witness the following: 'Fergus Slattery was superb on the pitch during matches; he led every training session: sprints, push-ups you name it – and he was a great man to party. He was last out of every reception but first to training next morning.

'Donal Lenihan was much the same as Slatts, bar the matches and the training.'

LABOUR OF LOVE

The lush tapestry of the GAA has been greatly enhanced by its cross-fertilisation with Irish rugby. One of Kerry's most famous sons, Dick Spring, was a noted Gaelic footballer. In fact, before he played rugby for Ireland he played football for Kerry.

As a boy his hero was Mick O'Connell, probably the greatest Gaelic footballer of them all. Spring claims that in Kerry they have taken and applied the words of the Olympic motto, 'Faster, Higher, Stronger' for their sporting heroes. As has been said of the Jesuits, 'They are tops in everything, including modesty.' But modesty is not something Kerry people have had much opportunity to experience.

Spring still follows club football in Kerry, like the progress of Laune Rangers. Back in the 1990s, someone said that they were the best side in Kerry since Tonto was their manager. This reminds Spring of the Galway wit who described an old Corinthians team as being the best since St Paul wrote to them.

In 1979 Spring was capped three times for the Irish rugby team. He is probably best remembered – though unfairly, as he was a much better player than he was given credit for – for an incident in the Wales match, when Ireland gifted the home side with fifteen points to lose on a scoreline of 24–21.

After twenty-two minutes Ireland led 6–0 courtesy of two lengthy penalties from Tony Ward. In the twenty-fifth minute the picture changed dramatically. The Welsh out-half lofted the kick towards the Irish posts, but Spring was under it and there seemed to be no danger. Somehow, the ball slipped through his hands and bounced over the Irish line for Allan Martin to rush on and score a try which Steve Fenwick converted. While his political career flourished in the 1980s and 1990s, he has never been let forget that incident and been the butt of jokes about 'a safe pair of hands'. Throughout the enormously popular series on RTÉ Radio One *Scrap Saturday* Spring was consistently referred to as 'Butterfingers' by Dermot Morgan, who went on to find fame as Father Ted. As a result, Spring always says that the highlight of his career was his first cap against France. That's the game he shows to his kids. He claims he can't remember what happened in the Wales game.

John Major was quite impressed when he heard Spring played for Ireland. Major played rugby himself when he was very young, but didn't prosper at the game because at that time he was too small, even though he is a tall man now. Major's great passion is cricket and his moods fluctuated a lot depending on the fate of the English team. Spring was always wary about having sensitive negotiations about the peace process in Northern Ireland with Major when England were playing. He found the best time to negotiate with Major was when England were doing very well at cricket. The only problem was that didn't happen very often.

McGann the Man

Barry McGann was one of the great Irish rugby fly-halves and a great soccer player. He was also a little 'calorifically challenged'. Around the time he was first capped for Ireland he moved from Cork to Dublin and was persuaded to play for Shelbourne. They had some tremendous players at the time like Ben Hannigan and Eric Barber. Barry always got a great slagging whenever he went back to play in Cork. One time they were playing Cork Celtic. As he ran onto the pitch he heard a voice saying on the terraces: 'Who's that fella?'

'That's McGann the rugby player.'

'Oh, wouldn't you know it by his stomach.'

An even more damning indictment of McGann's bulk was subsequently provided by Tony O'Reilly's quip: 'Twice around Barry McGann and you qualify as a bona fide traveller.'

Weighty Matters

Barry always had a bit of a problem with the battle of the bulge. Ray Gravell recalled his experiences of Barry for me: 'With Ollie

Campbell, another superb kicking out-half I came across for Ireland was Barry McGann. Barry was the fastest out-half I've ever seen over five yards. The problem is that he was completely f**ked after five yards.'

The classic comment though about Barry was: 'Given his waistline, the only thing that Barry McGann could ever dodge was a salad.'

One of Barry's great expressions was, 'He had two speeds – slow and very slow.'

WARM-UP

Asked about his outstanding memory from his Irish days, Barry McGann pauses only briefly.

'It was towards the final days of my international career. I was a sub for Mick Quinn at the time. Syd Millar was the coach then. I had the reputation of being a very laid-back player, but I was serious when I needed to be. Because of work I was late for a training session, although genuinely I got there as quickly as I could. The training session at Anglesea Road was in full swing when I arrived. I went over and apologised to Syd for being late and asked him what he wanted me to do. I had a strong feeling he didn't believe I had made much of an effort to be there, but he told me to warm-up. Instinctively I rubbed my hands together and blew on them and said: "Okay coach, I'm ready." Moss Keane was in stitches, but I'll never forget the bemused look on Syd's face. I think that incident probably cost me ten caps.'

FLY-ING LOW

McGann is a very genial man, and because of that features in a number of stories. He is known for his speed of thought. At the Lansdowne club dinner, the president droned on and on with his long-winded speech. The players were saying to each other, 'I wish there was a way to shut him up.'

'Leave it to me,' said McGann, who scribbled a note on a paper napkin and passed it up to the president, who read it, quickly finished his speech, and sat down.

'Brilliant,' said his teammates. 'What did you put in that note?'

Barry replied: 'Your fly is undone.'

MR PRESIDENT

The president of the club was retiring after many years of loyal service. At the dinner given in his honour by the club McGann rose to make his speech.

'It is said', he began, 'that when a child is born, its guardian angel gives it a kiss. If the kiss is on the hands, the child will become a musician or an artist. If the kiss is on the head, it will become a great thinker or scientist. If on the lips, it will grow up to be a singer or an actor. Now I don't know where our Bob here was kissed, but he's certainly been a damn good president.'

KICK EVERYTHING

Mick Quinn watched McGann at close quarters:

'Mike Gibson had a great temperament. The only time I ever saw him rattled was on the tour to New Zealand in 1976. We were really up against it in some of the matches. I remember Tom Grace saying at breakfast: "Quinner, do you think we'll get out of the place before they realise we're afraid of them?" We laughed at the time, but I wonder. Barry McGann did not share the general concern. He was playing at out-half that day and was kicking everything, and I mean everything. At one stage Gibbo yelled for a pass but Barry said: "Listen Mike, when I meet a player who can run as fast as I can kick it then I'll think about passing it."'

THE NUMBERS GAME

One of Barry's favourite stories goes back to Munster's All Blacks win:

'Tom Kiernan is an accountant by profession and has a great head for figures – most of the time at least. After the All Blacks were beaten by Munster in 1978 Tom, as their coach, was asked by a local journalist if it was a one-off. In all earnestness Kiernan is reputed to have replied: "You could play the All Blacks seven times and they would beat you nine times out of ten."'

TUCKING HELL

Colm Tucker was one of the stars of Munster's win over the All Blacks. Colm was also the source of amusement for his teammates, notably when Ireland played France at the Parc des Princes in 1980 – in the match programme his surname was spelt with an 'F' instead of a 'T'.

TOP OF THE PROPS

Like Moss Keane, Phil O'Callaghan was one of the great characters of the game. He toured three times with Irish parties; to Australia in 1967, to Argentina in 1970, and to New Zealand and Fiji in 1976. Apart from his fire on the pitch he was also noted for his quick wit. The most oft-quoted story about him is that of the day a referee penalised him and said: 'You're boring (as in describing the way a prop-forward drives in at an illegal angle into an opposing prop-forward), O'Callaghan.' Philo's instinctive retort was: 'Well, you're not so entertaining yourself, ref.' The referee penalised him a further ten yards.

Pregnant pause

During another match O'Callaghan put out his shoulder. The former Irish captain and leading gynaecologist Karl Mullen tended to him. Dr Mullen said: 'I'll put it back but I warn you it will be painful.' He did and it was. According to the story Philo was screaming his head off with the pain. The doctor turned to him and said: 'You should be ashamed of yourself. I was with a sixteen-year-old girl this morning in the Rotunda as she gave birth and there was not even a word of complaint from her.' Philo replied: 'I wonder what she bloody well would have said if you tried putting the f**kin' thing back in.'

The fear factor

Philo is famed for his experiences playing for Dolphin. The Old Wesley and Leinster player Bobby Macken joined Dolphin for a season. The following year he went back to Dublin. When he next played against Dolphin, Philo was standing on the wing as usual when Macken came charging towards him but to O'Callaghan's surprise he tapped the ball into touch. Philo asked him: 'Are you afraid of me Bobby?'

'No, but I'm afraid of running into your mouth,' he replied.

Solidarity

One of his strongest memories is of an incident involving Barry McGann:

'The night before an Irish squad session myself, McGann, Shay Deering and a couple of others had frequented a few pubs. In fact we were even thrown out of one of them. The squad session the next day started with some laps around the pitch. Shortly after we started off I heard Barry shout at me: "Cal, don't leave me." I dropped back with him and we were lapped once or twice. The cruel irony of the situation was that after the session he was selected and I was dropped.'

Deero

Apart from Moss Keane, Munster has never produced a player more loved by his peers than Shay Deering, as Tony Ward recalls:

'I just loved Shay and it was such a sadness when I heard that he passed away. Not just the rugby community but the world at large is a much poorer place without him.'

Shay had a keen sense of humour. He described the scene when one of his Garryowen teammates got married in the late 1970s. He laid down the following rules: 'I'll be home when I want and at what time I want – and I don't expect any hassle from you. I expect a great dinner to be on the table unless I tell you that I won't be home for dinner. I'll go playing rugby, training, hunting, fishing, boozing and card playing when I want with my teammates and don't you give me a hard time about it. Those are my rules. Any comments?'

His new bride said, 'No, that's fine with me. Just understand that there will be sex here at seven o'clock every night … whether you're here or not.'

At a party to mark his wedding anniversary, Shay was asked to give his friends a brief account of the benefits of marriage. Deero replied, 'Well, I've learned that marriage is the best teacher of all. It teaches you loyalty, forbearance, meekness, self-restraint, forgiveness – and a great many other qualities you wouldn't have needed if you'd stayed single.'

Happy days

Shay always enjoyed a good laugh with his fellow players. The size of the waistline of former Irish out-half Barry McGann was the subject of many a quip during his playing days. Shay joked that Barry joined an exclusive gym and spent about four hundred quid on it. He didn't lose a pound. He didn't realise that you have to show up to lose weight.

LEGAL EAGLE

Former Irish full back, and subsequent leader of the Irish Labour Party, Dick Spring was initially a lawyer by profession. Deering went to him in a professional capacity and stated, 'I would like to make a will but I don't know exactly how to go about it.'

Spring said, 'No problem, leave it all to me.'

Deero looked upset as he said, 'Well, I knew you were going to take the biggest slice, but I'd like to leave a little to my children, too.'

PROFESSIONAL COURTESY

Shay enjoyed a joke about lawyers at Spring's expense:

An engineer dies and reports to hell.

Pretty soon, the engineer gets dissatisfied with the level of comfort in hell, and starts designing and building improvements. After a while, they've got air conditioning and flush toilets and escalators, and the engineer becomes hugely popular. One day God calls the devil up on the telephone and says with a sneer, 'So, how's it going down there in hell?'

The devil replied, 'Things are going great. We've got air conditioning and flush toilets and escalators, and who knows what this engineer will come up with next.'

God replied, 'What? You've got an engineer? That's a mistake – he should never have gotten down there; send him up here.'

The devil said, 'No way. I like having an engineer on the staff, and I'm keeping him.'

God said, 'Send him back up here or I'll sue.'

Satan laughed uproariously and replied, 'Yeah, sure. And where are you going to get a lawyer?'

All creatures great and small

As a vet, Deero had a passionate interest in animal welfare. At one stage he met a rugby player from Mexico, of all places. He explained to Shay that rugby was a tiny, minority sport in Mexico, but that the number one sport was bullfighting.

The horrified Shay said, 'Isn't that revolting.'

'No,' the Mexican replied, 'revolting is our number two sport.'

One of Shay's favourite stories was about the dog who went into a hardware store and said: 'I'd like a job please.'

The hardware store owner said: 'We don't hire dogs, why don't you go join the circus?'

The dog replied: 'Well, what would the circus want with a plumber?'

A client took his Rottweiler to Shay.

'My dog's cross-eyed, is there anything you can do for him?'

'Well,' said Deero, 'let's have a look at him.'

So he picked the dog up and examined his eyes, then checked his teeth. Finally he said, 'I'm going to have to put him down.'

'What? Because he's cross-eyed?'

'No, because he's bloody heavy.'

Clean sweep

Cork Constitution has provided many Irish rugby legends down through the years, amongst them Tom Kiernan and Noel Murphy. One day, on a trip to England, they passed a shop and saw a notice on the window which read, 'Trousers £2. Shirts £1.50.' Tom and Noel were thrilled. They decided they would make a killing and buy them cheaply in England and sell them off at an increased price back home in Ireland. They decided to play it cool and speak in English accents. When they went in they calmly walked up to the counter and said to the manager, 'We'll buy all the trousers and shirts you have.'

The manager looked at them with astonishment. Despite their feigned accents he asked, 'Excuse me gentlemen are you both from Cork?'

Noel and Tom asked in unison, 'How did you know?'

'Oh, call it an inspired guess. You probably didn't notice, but this is actually a dry cleaners.'

LOST IN TRANSLATION

Tom Kiernan was renowned for his quickness of thought. Hence his nickname 'the Grey Fox'. This was probably best typified on the 1968 Lions tour when the young Gareth Edwards was getting irate with the decisions of the referee. He went so far as to call him 'a cheating f**ker'. The ref told Edwards he was sending him off for bad language. As captain, Kiernan intervened and asked the ref what the problem was. With more than a hint of impatience the ref remarked acidly: 'Your scrum half called me a f**ker and I'm sending him off.'

Kiernan soothingly calmed him down: 'He certainly wasn't. He was talking Welsh to his out-half partner.'

The referee was immediately placated and rescinded his decision, and Edwards continued to play on. And who was his out-half? None other than Mike Gibson, who didn't speak a word of Welsh.

TOM AND NOISY

Tom Kiernan was a great motivator. He coached Munster to their win over the All Blacks in 1978 and Ireland to their Triple Crown win in 1982. Before Munster played Australia in 1967 the team met in the Metropole hotel. Noel 'Noisy' Murphy limped in before the match and said, 'My leg is shagged and I can't play.' A sub was duly called for and informed of his selection. Then Kiernan cut loose with his motivational speech. Everyone was ready to tear into the Aussies afterwards. Noel Murphy was so caught up by Kiernan's emotion that he said, 'Ara, f**k it Tom, I'll play.'

DRIVE SAFELY

John Robbie retains a funny memory of Noel Murphy from his time as Lions manager in 1979:

'Jean Pierre Rives, the celebrated French flanker, was there as well at the end of the tour. I was in Pretoria with Noel Murphy at some function or other, and we got a lift back with some bloke in a sports car who was taking Jean Pierre back to Johannesburg. We got hopelessly lost, and I recall that as we sped at breakneck speed down a back road we could see a fork ahead. "Go left," said Noel to the driver. "Please go right," said I. "Please go f**king slower!" screamed Rives, who could speak little English, from the back seat. The driver, a South African, was laughing so hard he nearly crashed.'

TAKING THE MICK

In his full life Mick English was immortalised around the world in after dinner speeches by Tony O'Reilly. Playing against Phil Horrocks-Taylor during a Wolfhounds match in Limerick, English was asked what he thought of his opponent who had scored a try that day. English replied: 'Well, Horrocks went one way, Taylor the other and I was left with the hyphen.' In the O'Reilly version though this exchange happened after an Ireland–England international at Twickenham. English never played opposite Horrocks-Taylor in an international.

English was tickled by a letter written to him by the late Mai Purcell of *The Limerick Leader* when he won his first cap. The letter read:

Mick. I should like to impress on you that I'm spending a whole week's wages to visit Dublin just to see you play and I beseech you not to make an idiot of yourself on this occasion.

I furthermore request that on this auspicious occasion be mindful of your duties and responsibilities not only to your club and the people of Limerick but to your country as a whole, and that you keep your bloody eye on the ball. Good luck and God Bless.

ALARM-ING

No one had a greater passion for rugby in Limerick than Tom Clifford. He was first capped for Ireland against France in 1949, and was a key part of the Triple Crown victory in that season and toured with the Lions to New Zealand in 1950. He was one of nine Irish players to make the tour with Karl Mullen, George Norton, Michael Lane, Noel Henderson, Jack Kyle, Jimmy Nelson, Billy McKay and Jim McCarthy.

His name lives on through 'Tom Clifford Park', a ground which had been variously described as 'The Killing Fields', 'The Garden of Get Somebody' and 'Jurassic Park'.

At Tom's funeral the church was teeming with rugby folk. The priest giving the homily had been a lifelong friend of Tom's, and told the congregation how he had once invited the giant of Irish rugby to his ordination Mass. After the ceremony he asked Tom what he thought of it. Tom replied, 'You spoke too long. The next time if you go on for longer than ten minutes I'll set off an alarm clock in the church.' The next Sunday the priest saw Tom arriving in at the church and noticed he had a bulge in his overcoat. When Tom caught his eye, he pulled out an alarm clock.

BIG TOM

Tom won the last of his fourteen caps against France in 1952, a match that also saw the end of the international careers of Karl Mullen, Des O'Brien and Bill McKay.

According to legend, Tom's rugby affiliation was evident at an early age. When he was in primary school he got a new teacher who came from a different part of Limerick and as a result she was a fanatical Shannon fan. On her first day she asked Tom what team he supported. Tom replied, 'Young Munster.'

'And why do you support Young Munster?'

'Because my mum and dad support them.'

'And I suppose if your parents were Shannon fans you would be a Shannon supporter.'

'No Miss. If my parents were Shannon fans I would be an idiot.'

<h2 style="text-align:center">A GOOD PROP-OSITION</h2>

For Jim McCarthy, Clifford was not only one of the great props but perhaps the greatest character in Irish rugby:

'I was on the Lions tour with Tom in 1950. Tom was a larger-than-life figure, especially when he sang his party piece "O'Reilly's Daughter". His only rival in the character stakes was probably Cliff Davies, a Welsh coalminer. Cliff was greeted by the New Zealand Prime Minister, Sidney Holland, who said: "Glad to meet you, Cliff." Cliff retorted: "Glad to meet you, Sid."'

<h2 style="text-align:center">A NEW JOB</h2>

Having successfully negotiated the Lions tour, Clifford was immediately involved in an accident when he returned to Ireland. He took a taxi in Dublin and, anxious to ask the taxi driver if he knew what time the next train was to Limerick, he leaned forward and tapped the driver on the shoulder. The driver screamed, lost control of the cab, nearly hit a bus, drove up over a footpath, and stopped just inches from a large plate glass window. For a few moments everything was silent in the taxi. The startled Clifford apologised to the driver, saying he didn't realise a mere tap on the shoulder would frighten him so much.

'No, no,' the driver replied. 'It's all my fault. Today is my first day driving a taxi. For the last twenty-five years I've been driving a hearse.'

THE KILLING FIELDS

Tom even enjoyed the joke told by visiting teams from Dublin:

'Why does the Shannon run through Limerick?'

'Would you walk through Limerick?'

Tom's legend lives on in rugby folklore. On the Lions tour Clifford warned some of the Welsh players about the hazards of going out with an Irish Catholic girl on the basis that you could take the girl out of Cork but …

DOPEY

Tom was adept at psyching his team up for English games in particular. He once told the team about the three young children who went to heaven, but God said they were too young to die. He told them to take a run off the cloud and on the way back down to Earth to shout out what they wanted to be. The first lad jumped and said he wanted to be a successful teacher. Twenty years later he was the youngest head teacher in the country. The second wanted to be a successful lawyer, and twenty years later he was the youngest judge ever appointed. The third young lad tripped over his own feet jumping off the cloud and involuntarily shouted out: 'Clumsy bast**d.' Twenty years later he was playing scrum half for England.

REVERSE PSYCHOLOGY

Tom had a great capacity to outpsych his opponents. Before an international against England, he went up to the two English props and said: 'I'm very sorry. I just heard the news. You don't deserve that – either of you.'

The two English players were puzzled: 'What do you mean?'

'I've just heard what everybody's calling the two of you.'

'Really? We haven't heard anything. So what are people calling us behind our backs?'

'Sim-bolic.'

'Symbolic? Why are they calling us that?'

Tom paused theatrically before replying: 'Cos one of you is simple and the other is a bo***x.'

DEATH WISH

The Wallabies toured the British Isles in 1948. Things heated up when they played Munster. Munster had a very simple way of dealing with touring sides – to bring them down to their level as soon as possible, and then it was an even match. Nick Shehadie, one of the stars of the Australian side, was confronted by Tom Clifford. Shehadie was a bit taken aback by the opening greeting: 'Come in here son. You may as well die here as in f**kin' Sydney.'

After the match Shehadie was told that one of his opponents was getting married the following day. 'Congratulations, my boy,' said Shehadie. 'I'm sure you will look back on today as the happiest day of your life.'

'But I'm not getting married until tomorrow,' protested the young player.

'I know,' said Shehadie.

DOCTOR'S ORDERS

A club team from Limerick was on tour in New Zealand. The fly-half was a Tom Cruise lookalike, and was a big hit with all the ladies at the many parties they attended. One night he struck up a relationship with a Nicole Kidman lookalike, and she brought him home and took him to bed. They were in the throes of passion when the woman's husband walked in. 'What the hell do you think you're doing?' he screamed.

'I'm ... er ... I'm a doctor and I'm ... taking your wife's temperature,' stammered the fly-half.

'Right,' said the husband. 'I hope for your sake that thing's got numbers on it when you take it out.'

RUGBY SPIRITS IN THE SKY

During an interpro match there was a lightning strike and both Brian O'Driscoll and Paul O'Connell were sadly killed. They ascended into heaven and, given their status in the rugby hierarchy, they bypassed St Peter at the Pearly Gates and were brought in the VIP entrance where they were greeted by no less than God himself. 'Greetings. Heaven is enriched by having both of you here. Come, I will show your accommodation. I hope you'll both be comfortable.'

God took Brian by the hand, and led him off on a short walk through beautiful fields of flowers until they came across a pretty thatched cottage by a stream, with a beautiful garden, lovely flower beds and tall trees swaying in the gentle breeze. The thatched roof the shades of the tricolour, the birds in the trees were whistling 'Ireland's Call', and the gnomes by the garden path were images of great Leinster rugby heroes: Ollie Campbell, Jamie Heaslip, Phil Orr, and Karl Mullen.

O'Driscoll was left uncharacteristically speechless. Eventually he muttered, 'I don't know what to say.'

God then took O'Connell up the path. As they were strolling away, Bod looked around him and, further up the road, he saw a gigantic mansion. On the manicured lawns, there were huge 20ft golden statues of Munster legends Moss Keane, Keith Wood, Peter Clohessy, Ronan O'Gara and John Hayes, overlooking a beautiful, magnificent garden. Massed choirs of birds were singing 'Stand Up and Fight' in a harmony that the Everly Brothers would have marvelled at. A little flustered, Drico ran after God and his old rival, tapped God on the shoulder and said: 'Excuse me God, I don't wish to sound ungrateful or anything, but I was wondering why Paul's house is so much more stylish than mine.'

God smiled beatifically at him and said: 'There there, Brian, don't worry, it's not Paul's house. It's mine.'

CHAPTER FOUR

Leinster Legends

Trevor Brennan brought great freshness to the Leinster squad. There are lots of stories about Trevor, and indeed other Leinster greats, and this chapter features many of them.

GIRV THE SWERVE

Girvan Dempsey's favourite story has a linguistic theme:

'Trevor was responsible for my funniest moment in rugby. It was one of my first starts for Leinster and we were playing Treviso on a pre-season tour in Italy. After we flew into the airport and collected our bags our manager at the time, Jim Glennon, came in to tell us there would be a delay because there was a difficulty with Dean Oswald's passport. The problem was compounded by the fact that there was a language barrier. Trevor immediately piped up: "I'll sort it out for you. I know the lingo." We were all stunned because Trevor was not known for his linguistic skills. When we asked him when he had learned to speak Italian he coolly replied: "I worked in Luigi's chip shop one summer."'

A TOUCH OF CLASS

Former Leinster manager and rugby raconteur Ken Ging tells a classic Brennan story:

'One day, Sir Anthony O'Reilly was driving home in his brand new Rolls Royce. He was smiling because it was the most magnificent model. He pulled up beside a tiny car at a traffic lights, with a black cloud of smoke trailing from the exhaust and black tape on a few of the windows. Trevor Brennan gets out from the mini and walks up to O'Reilly and signals to him to roll down the window. The Lions legend duly does so and Trevor asks: "Do you have a telephone in there, Anto?"

O'Reilly replied: "I have."

"Do you have a TV and a DVD player?"

"I do and before you ask I've also got a fully stocked cocktail bar."

"Have you a bed?"

"I haven't a bed."

Trevor replies, "I've a bed in my car", and walked off.

This really got to O'Reilly. The following day he instructed his personal assistant to get a four poster bed installed in his car. A few minutes later the secretary returned and explained to O'Reilly that this would cost a fortune. O'Reilly snapped back angrily: "I don't care. Just get me that bed."

Two weeks later, O'Reilly was driving home and feeling really proud of his state-of-the-art bed, with beautiful satin sheets. However, he was somewhat dejected because he thought he would never see Trevor again to show him his new prize possession. He pulled into a Tesco to buy his groceries and to his great delight he spotted Trevor's mini in the car park. He walked over and knocked at the window. After a long pause, Trevor pulled down the window and said: "Ah, Anto it's yourself."

O'Reilly was nearly jumping for joy: "Trevor, Trevor, let me show you the great new bed I have installed in my car."

Brennan shook his head and looked at him scornfully: "Do you mean to tell me you dragged me out of the shower just to show me a bed?"'

THE STREETS OF DUBLIN

The most famous Trevor tale goes back to the day he was walking down Dublin City Centre when he saw a man dead on the street. He pulled out his mobile phone and rang the Gardaí. He told the garda the situation and the boy in blue replied, 'Okay you're there in Exchequer Street. Spell Exchequer Street.'

Trevor started, 'E, x, c … no … e, x, h … no …' He paused and said, 'Hang on a second. I'm just going to drag him round to Dame Street and I'll ring you back then.'

HANGING ON THE TELEPHONE

One story about Trevor goes back to the time when he was a little boy and answered the phone. A man asked, 'Hello, is your Dad around?'

Trevor whispered, 'Yes.'

The man then asked if he could talk to him.

'He's busy at the moment,' Brennan whispered.

'Then is your Mom there?'

'Yes,' the boy whispered.

'Can I talk to her?'

'No, she's busy,' Trevor whispered.

'Is there anyone else there?'

'Yes,' whispered little Trevor.

'Who?'

'A policeman,' came the whispered reply.

'Well, can I talk to him?'

'He's busy too,' Trevor whispered.

Annoyed, the man asked what they were all doing.

'Looking for me,' Brennan whispered.

MILLER'S CROSSING

Munster faced Leinster in the inaugural Celtic League final in Lansdowne Road. Eric Miller was sent off after only twenty minutes, but Leinster won the final nonetheless. Afterwards, in the Leinster dressing room, Eric was distraught. Sensing his pain, his teammates rallied and one by one went to console him. Finally, it was Trevor's turn. He grabbed a pale-faced Miller roughly by the shoulders and said: 'If we'd lost that game you wouldn't be safe in Tora-f**king-Bora.'

EAR TO THE GROUND

Leinster legend Felipe Contepomi enjoys the many stories that are told about Irish rugby. One involves the former Irish prop-forward who was hurt very badly during a scrum and had both of his ears ripped off. Since he was permanently disfigured, he decided to give up playing rugby for good. His club and insurance company ensured that a large sum of money went his way.

One day he decided to invest his money in a small but growing sportswear business. He bought the company outright but after signing on the dotted line, realised that he knew nothing about business. He decided to employ someone to run the shop.

The next day he set up three interviews. The first guy was great. He knew everything he needed to know and was very enthusiastic. At the end of the interview, the ex-Irish international asked him, 'Do you notice anything different about me?'

And the man replied, 'Why, yes, I couldn't help noticing you have no ears.' The rugby player got angry and threw him out.

The second interview was with a woman, and she was even better than the first guy. He asked her the same question, 'Do you notice anything different about me?'

She replied: 'Well, you have no ears.' He got upset again and showed her the door.

The third and final interviewee was the best of the three. He was a very young man, fresh out of college. He was smart and handsome, and seemed to know all about the sportswear business.

The rugby player was anxious, but went ahead and asked him the same question: 'Do you notice anything different about me?'

To his surprise the young man answered: 'Yes, you wear contact lenses.'

The interviewer was taken aback and asked: 'How do you know that I wear contacts?'

The interviewee retorted: 'It's obvious. You have no f**king ears to wear glasses.'

MATT-ER OF FACT

With the retirement of Ian McGeechan after the 2003 World Cup, Matt Williams was appointed Scottish coach, having enjoyed great success with Leinster. He should have known the magnitude of the task when BBC commentator Nick Mullins noted that his selection was akin to 'rearranging deck chairs on the Titanic'.

Williams is one of the increasing number of coaches who have made the journey from 'down under' to Britain and Ireland, having started his coaching career with New South Wales in Australia. Many people are unhappy with the growing influence of Aussies on Scottish rugby, not just at the coaching level but also amongst the playing community. The former Scottish international John Beattie jokes that such is the current Aussie influence on Scottish rugby that Murrayfield will have to be rechristened 'Ramsay Street' after the celebrated street in Australia's most famous soap, *Neighbours*.

Williams once described the cultural differences between Ireland and France. 'In Ireland they take you to parties and give you loads of free drink in the pubs, then kick the daylights out of you on the pitch. They do the same in France, except they don't take you to parties or give you free drink in the pubs.'

HAIL THE PROPHET

It is said that when a prominent former All Black (who shall remain nameless because of the libel laws) dies, the presiding clergyman will have to break with liturgical convention. Such is his liking for publicity that instead of saying 'May perpetual light shine upon him' the vicar will probably say: 'May perpetual *limelight* shine upon him.'

At the opposite end of the modesty spectrum is Ollie Campbell. He shows the same discomfort with generous compliments that the Pope would be expected to show in a brothel.

One of Campbell's gifts is that he can predict the future: 'A number of years ago I was coaching Belvedere's under-8s. We played Naas and lost narrowly. The lads were devastated. I told them not to worry because we would be playing them again before the end of the season and would beat them then. We won the return fixture and one of the boys came up to me and with awe in his voice said: "You can tell the future."

'I commiserated with the Naas coach and he asked me what I thought of his team. I told him they were a good side and said: "The blonde fellow is one to watch." He was Jamie Heaslip.'

CAMPBELL'S KINGDOM

After he was sensationally dropped by the Irish rugby selectors on the tour to Australia in 1979, Tony Ward became embroiled in one of the most keenly argued controversies in the history of Irish sport. For three years a fierce debate raged: who should wear Ireland's number ten jersey, Tony Ward or Ollie Campbell?

Ollie Campbell thought he had finally resolved the Tony Ward issue with a series of stunning performances that ensured Ireland broke a thirty-three-year famine and won the Triple Crown in 1982. A few weeks later, Ollie was leaving Westport when he picked up an elderly lady who was visiting a friend in Castlebar Hospital. After an initial flurry of small talk the conversation unfolded as follows:

Her: 'And what sports do you play? Do you play Gaelic?'

Ollie (as modestly as possible): 'No, I play rugby?'

Long silence.

Her: 'Do you know, there's one thing I'll never understand about rugby.'

Ollie (with all due modesty): 'What? I might be able to help.'

Short silence.

Her: 'The only thing I don't understand about rugby is why Tony Ward is not on the Irish team.'

HOLY SHOW

In 1984, Ollie found himself the main topic of conversation amongst the chattering classes. When he pulled out of the England game that year it was suggested by some that he was giving up rugby and joining the priesthood. He has absolutely no idea where this particular rumour emanated from. To this day though, former Irish scrum half John Robbie still calls him Fr Campbell.

To highlight just how absurd that fabricated story was, two weeks later, after Ireland played Scotland, Ollie turned up to the post-match dinner dressed as a priest. Not only that, but he persuaded a female friend of his to accompany him dressed up as a nun. He went around all night with a fag in one hand (and he has never smoked), a pint in the other (and at the time he didn't drink) and danced away with this 'nun' (although he has never been much of a dancer). All of this was so out of character for him that he assumed people would immediately see that the priesthood story was entire nonsense. What staggered him was the amount of people who came to him and – apologising to 'sister' for interrupting – sincerely congratulated him on his big decision. Instead of putting this little fire out, all he succeeded in doing was pouring more fuel on it.

THE LIVE MIKE

Even after his retirement from rugby Campbell still found his name linked with Tony Ward's. He was invited onto Mike Murphy's radio show and before the broadcast the producer asked if there were any subjects he did not wish to discuss. He said: 'Tony Ward and South Africa', because he thought they had been flogged to death. The first question Mike asked him was: 'I see here Ollie that the two things that you said you don't want to be questioned about are South Africa and Tony Ward. Why is that?'

SHOCK AND AWE

Ollie Campbell was at the height of his fame after Ireland won the Triple Crown in 1982 – for the first time in thirty-three years. A young neighbour, who was six at the time, wanted his autograph. He arrived reasonably early before Ollie went out and he had been psyching himself up for this moment for weeks. He was obviously expecting his hero to arrive at the door wearing a jersey, togs and boots, with a rugby ball under his arm, because when Ollie appeared all the boy could blurt out with a tone of absolute shock was, 'You wear clothes!'

FISHY STORY

Hugo MacNeill is a good friend and huge admirer of Ollie Campbell's, but he enjoys stories which reflect his illustrious teammate in a poor light. A notable example is the one where Campbell goes on a fishing holiday with Willie Duggan. They rented a boat and fished on a lake every day. After six days they still had not caught anything, but on the seventh day they caught thirty fish. Ollie said to Willie, 'Mark this spot so that we can come back here again tomorrow.'

The next day, when they were driving to rent the boat, Campbell asked Duggan, 'Did you mark that spot?'

Willie replied, 'Yeah, I put a big X on the bottom of the boat.'

Ollie said, 'You stupid fool … what if we don't get that same boat today?'

SUPERMAC

Ollie's biggest problem is that he can't say no when people ask him to do them a favour. Hugo MacNeill rang him up one night, put on an accent and told him he was Mick Fitzgerald from Irish Marketing Ltd. He said he was organising a beauty competition for nurses and that he wanted him to be one of the judges, knowing full well that Ollie would hate that kind of thing. He sighed and sighed, struggling to come up with a plausible excuse. Eventually Ollie asked what date the contest was on. When Hugo gave him the date Ollie said, 'Oh that's an awful shame. I'm really sorry but I have another function on that night. It's such a pity because I always wanted to judge a beauty contest.'

'That's no problem Ollie. You see, one of the prizes we are going to offer is a night out with Ollie Campbell. We'll pay for everything and it'll be first class all the way.'

'Gosh, I'm afraid I'm going to have a lot of commitments around that time. I won't have many nights free.'

'But that's the beauty of this Ollie; we'll arrange it for any night that suits you.'

The panic was getting ever more noticeable in Ollie's voice and Hugo could visualise him writhing in his chair as he tried to find a way to back out of it. Eventually, Ollie said he was backing away from that type of thing. Then Hugo asked him if there were any of his colleagues who would be willing to do that kind of thing. Ollie blurted out Hugo's name immediately and provided his phone number faster than you could say Tony Ward.

SUBS BENCH

Hugo told me he was himself the victim of a good put-down: 'I was down in Cork with Moss Finn, Donal Lenihan and Michael Kiernan and we were having lunch with five or six rugby fans. In any other place in Ireland sports fans would have passed the time by picking their greatest ever Irish team. Not so in Cork. They picked the worst ever Irish team. I kept my head down as they discussed my position, expecting to have my name mentioned at any minute. After they made their choice for full back I remarked with relief: "I suppose I can relax now." Quick as a flash someone said: "Hang on, we haven't picked the subs yet."'

SLEEPING PARTNERS

When he burst onto the Irish team Hugo was in awe of Willie Duggan. In 1985, following Duggan's retirement, their relationship was more like that of two equals. Hugo promised to get Willie tickets for the Scotland match. He was sharing a room with Brian Spillane and the phone rang the night before the match. Hugo answered with the words, 'The Spillane–MacNeill suite.' Immediately he heard Willie respond, 'You might as well be sleeping together you spend so much time together on the pitch.'

DEANO

Hugo's teammate with Leinster and Ireland was Paul Dean. Deano shared his fondest rugby memories with me:

'A great character I became friendly with was the Scottish international John Jeffrey. He became a good friend of mine. The night before we played Scotland in 1985 we went to the cinema, as was the tradition back then. All I remember of the film was that it starred Eddie Murphy and his catchphrase was: "Get the f**k out of here." As soon as the film was over the lights came on and when we stood up we saw that the Scottish team were sitting three rows behind us. We had a popcorn fight with them, which was great fun, and they started shouting at us: "Get the f**k out of here." Almost as soon as the match started the next day John Jeffrey tackled me very late. He knew exactly what he was doing. It was too early in the game for him to be penalised. As he pinned me down on the ground he whispered in my ear: "Get the f**k out of here." The nice thing was that we did get the f**k out of there – but with a victory.'

SCOTTISH PASSION

Dean enjoys the story about the young John Jeffrey and his first girlfriend. They were sitting on a low stone wall, holding hands and gazing out over the loch. For several minutes they sat silently, then finally she looked at the future Scottish legend and said, 'A penny for your thoughts, John.'

'Well, uh, I was thinking … perhaps it's about time for a wee kiss.'

The girl blushed, then leaned over and kissed him lightly on the cheek. Then he blushed.

Then the two turned once again to gaze out over the loch. After a while the girl spoke again. 'Another penny for your thoughts, John.'

The young Jeffrey knit his brow. 'Well, now,' he said, 'my thoughts are a bit more serious this time.'

'Really?' said the girl in a whisper, filled with anticipation.

'Aye,' said Jeffrey. 'Don't you think it's about time you paid me that first penny.'

WITH A LITTLE HELP FROM MY FRIENDS

There is one former teammate whose name elicits a very animated response from Dean.

'When I started with Ireland, I loved playing with Michael

Kiernan because he was so fast. However, as he got older he put on weight and started to lose his speed. My job was to make our talented backline look good. The problem was that I made Michael look much, much better than he actually was.'

Many rugby fans felt Michael Kiernan left the Irish team prematurely. For the first time, Deano can exclusively reveal the real reason for Kiernan's premature retirement. 'He left because of illness. The truth is, everyone was sick of him.'

However, he very reluctantly denies that he christened Kiernan 'Pepper' because he always got up your nose.

Captain's call

Not surprisingly, Kiernan features in Deano's personal favourite rugby story:

'Michael Kiernan was always a terribly bad influence on me. After we lost badly at home to England one year we went to the post-match dinner in the Shelbourne. Will Carling was the young, up-and-coming captain of England. It was one of his first games as captain. There were three hundred people there, all men. It was black tie only, and a bit stuffy. We were looking forward to having a few beers after the game. At the Shelbourne there were waiters going around with double gin and tonics on silver trays at the reception before the dinner. Will Carling arrived in a white dinner jacket with his hair gelled back. Everybody else was wearing a black suit. Michael and I steered Will into a corner, grabbed a silver tray full of G and Ts and toasted Will, many times, on England's success. We had been drinking before the reception and were getting pretty sloshed. Will's mistake was to think that because we were senior players he was safe with us. The English manager was Roger Uttley and he had been looking for Will. When he found us, he grabbed him and took him away, saying forcefully to him: "You're captain of England. You have to be careful. You have responsibilities. You have to give a speech."

'The dinner was structured with English and Irish players around circular tables. I was completely dwarfed sitting between Paul Ackford and Wade Dooley. It was a very stuffy environment and so before the dinner we entertained ourselves with drinking games. The problem was that we were terrible drinkers. Roger Uttley was minding Carling for the meal, but during the dinner Will slipped away from him and he came down to us from the top table and sat down between Paul Ackford and myself. The English players were not too happy with Will wearing a white dinner jacket as well, being very prim and proper. We pushed him under the table and closed in our seats. It was a big table, and Will was under the middle of it shouting: "Lads, let me out." His voice could not be heard in the noisy room though.

'Uttley was looking frantically for him because it was coming close to the speeches. Will started kicking us to get out. We couldn't see him so we started kicking him back. The next drink was a glass of red wine, so in uniformity, one after the other, we threw it under the table on top of his white dinner jacket and gelled hair. Will started screaming, "Lads, let me out or I'll turn over the table." We all put our elbows on the table. We were laughing away, and eventually Roger saw what was going on and dragged Will out from under the table. There were big, red wine stains dripping off his lovely white jacket. A few minutes later Will gave his speech. Carling subsequently went on to make a fortune going around to companies giving inspirational speeches, but let's just say his address that night wasn't his finest moment.'

WINGING IT

Former Irish winger Freddie McLennan was the ultimate practical joker. In 1980, when Leinster toured Romania, Paul Dean was making his provincial debut on the tour and was desperate to become one of the 'lads'. At dinner one night, Paul McNaughton asked Deano to go up to Freddie and ask him what size shoes did his mother wear. Paul was a bit suspicious, but eventually agreed to do so. As soon as he did, Freddie turned away and put his hand over his face and started to sob. Deano didn't know what to make of this and asked some of the other players what was the matter. They replied: 'Did you not know? Freddie's mother was in a horrific car crash a fortnight ago and had both her feet amputated.' Deano's face turned a whiter shade of pale and a number of times he tried to apologise to Freddie that night but every time he got near him some of the players headed him off. It was well into the night before Deano found out that it was all a con job and he had fallen for it hook, line and sinker.

COME DINE WITH ME

On that tour to Romania in 1980 Dean was soon fed up with the food on offer. On a bus journey, the two big jokers in the side, Paul McNaughton and Freddie McLennan, walked up to him with a list taking the lunch orders. Deano was told he could choose between T-bone steak or grilled chicken, and he had to indicate whether he wanted chips, baked or sautéed potatoes, and select from a choice of vegetables, as it all had to be ordered in advance. Deano got very excited, and took great care over the menu. He arrived at an impressive looking restaurant for a big meal with a buzz of expectancy – which turned into a stunned silence when the food arrived. Each dish was the same: a big bowl of clear, greasy soup and in it was a huge fish head complete with eyes. Deano could eat nothing. McNaughton and McLennan had to be led out – they were laughing so much they couldn't walk. Deano's tears were of a different variety.

ICE, ICE FREDDIE

Johnny Moloney, however, once saw the tables turned on McLennan:

'Mick Quinn would sometimes involve me as his partner in crime. He had this trick he played on every player gaining his first cap. A lot of players before their debut start to feel that they are a bit sluggish and not at their best. Quinny would pretend to be very sympathetic and tell them he had the solution. He would inform them in the strictest confidence that the top players always took a freezing cold bath to give them an edge in a big match. The only reason this was not generally known was that it was a trade secret.

'The biggest casualty in all of this was Freddie McLennan. We put him in a cold bath and added buckets of ice. We told him he had to wait in there for twenty minutes, otherwise it was no good. He was squealing like a pig. When his time was up he couldn't move and had ice on his legs.'

STYLE ICON

Colin Patterson was a big fan of McLennan:

'Freddie is a great personality. Once when we played England, Freddie and John Carleton were having a real jousting match. At one stage John sent Freddie crashing to the ground in a tackle. As he was going back to his position Freddie shouted at him: "John, John. Is my hair all right?" If you watch the video of the game you'll see John cracking up with laughter and Freddie straightening his hair.'

PHONE IN

Terry Kennedy won the first of his thirteen caps on the wing for Ireland against Wales in 1978. He toured South Africa with Ireland in 1981. Before the tour, John Robbie was called into his boss' office (he worked for Guinness) and told that he was not allowed to go. Robbie resigned, even though he was married, with a young child to support. He still retained his sense of humour through this difficult time.

'The great departure day arrived, and then we learnt about the cloak-and-dagger methods that we were going to use to get to South Africa. I suppose it was necessary, and we were getting worried about running the gauntlet at Dublin airport, as we'd heard that a massive demonstration had been planned. I rang Terry Kennedy, and in my best Peter Sellers Indian accent I told him that I was Kadar Asmal, the high profile leader of the Irish anti-apartheid movement, and could I talk to him? Terry was very worried and when I asked him to confirm some secret arrangements for our departure, I could almost see the beads of sweat pouring from his brow. He was gibbering like an idiot and nearly collapsed in relief when I told him it was me.'

A PASSAGE TO ROMANIA

In 1980, the year Jimmy Carter had arranged a boycott of the Moscow Olympics because of Russia's invasion of Afghanistan, Leinster, under Mick Doyle and Mick 'the Cud' Cuddy, toured Romania. The Cud was a master of the art of the misnomer. One of his many classic comments is: 'There were so many people they were coming out of the woodworm.'

PUT YOUR BACK(SIDE) INTO IT

One of the players on the tour was Jim Glennon, who in 2002 was elected a T.D. As a player Jim always gave 150 per cent. Although he is not an arrogant person he does make one proud boast: 'Nobody used his arse better in the line-out than Jim Glennon did.'

Glennon was never a great line-out winner, but was very hard to get line-out ball from. He formed a very effective second row partnership with George Wallace for Leinster. They were christened 'Urbi et Orbi' by Mick Doyle.

QUICK THINKING

Jim was also known for his shrewd man-management. One of the stories is about the way he dealt with a Leinster player who had a very high opinion of himself and a fondness for the good life, but who was not noted for his intelligence. The team were flying off on tour to Italy and were travelling in economy class. The player in question saw that the first class seats appeared to be much larger and more comfortable and he moved forward to the last empty one. The stewardess checked his ticket and told the player that his seat was in economy. The Leinster player insisted he was not moving. Flustered, the stewardess went back to the cockpit and informed the captain of the problem. The captain went back and told the player that his assigned seat was in economy. A heated row developed. Seeing the commotion Glennon assured the pilot he would handle the situation. He then briefly whispered something into the player's ear. He immediately got up, said, 'Thank you so much, Jim,' shook hands with Glennon and rushed back to his seat in the economy section. The captain was watching with rapt attention and asked Glennon what he had said to the player.

Jim replied, 'I just told him that the first class section wasn't going to Italy.'

SOCIABLE

Jim Glennon was involved in Mick Doyle's first and last representative games as coach – in 1979 when Leinster played Cheshire and in 1987 when Ireland played Australia. He lays claim to an unusual distinction – he once saw Doyle speechless. After his heart attack during the 1987 World Cup, Doyler rejoined the Irish team after a ten day stay in hospital. They were staying in a motel type place. A few of the lads, known on the tour as the 'amigos', were out late one night and sneaking furtively in. There was an uncarpeted stairs outside Doyler's room and he was woken up by the activity. He recognised one of the voices. The next day the culprit was given a right ticking off in front of the whole squad. As Doyler delivered his attack the player in question stood and listened but when the coach had finished the bad boy said: 'Jaysus Doyler, there's none so pure as a converted hoor.' Doyler was left too stunned to speak.

CAPTAIN FANTASTIC

Stories about Willie Duggan abound. Like Moss Keane, he was an Irish national institution. A man with little enthusiasm for training, his most celebrated comment was 'Training takes the edge off my game.' Duggan was one of a rare group of players who always made a point of bringing a pack of cigarettes with him onto the training field. Asked once in a radio interview if this was a major problem for him fitness-wise, he took the broadcaster by surprise by saying that it was a positive advantage: 'Sure if it wasn't for the fags I would be offside all day long.'

CHESTY

There was an inherent contradiction in Duggan's preparation for matches. He always had a cigarette five minutes before going out onto the pitch, then he took out a jar of Vicks and rubbed it on his chest. To put it mildly, he had an unconventional approach.

HOT STUFF

Willie turned up for training with the Irish squad and when he was told to warm-up he replied: 'I don't need to. I had the heater on in the car.'

Tired and emotional

Willie was finding it difficult to train with his club team, Blackrock. It was agreed, at Irish hooker John Cantrell's suggestion, that one Sunday the entire squad would go down to Kilkenny Rugby Club to facilitate Willie because he lived there. That morning they were all there bar one … Willie. Somebody had to go and wake him because he had slept it out.

Unorthodox

Donal Lenihan told me of his admiration for Willie Duggan:

'The best Irish forward I ever played with was Willie Duggan. He was the Scarlet Pimpernel of Irish rugby because he was so hard to find for training. Having said that, he wouldn't have survived in international rugby so long without training. Willie took his captaincy manual from a different world. His speeches were not comparable with anything I'd ever heard before or since.

'One of my clearest memories of Willie's captaincy is of the morning after the Scotland game in 1984. The papers all had a picture of Duggan with his arm around Tony Ward and speaking to him. It was just before Wardy was taking a penalty. It appeared that Willie was acting the real father figure, but knowing him as I do my guess was he was saying: "If you miss this penalty, I'll kick you all the way to Kilkenny."'

Snoring Beauty

Ireland's tour to Australia in 1979 provided perhaps the funniest moment in Ollie Campbell's rugby career:

'The night before the first Test we had a team meeting. Our coach, Noel "Noisy" Murphy, always got very worked up when he spoke at these meetings. The problem was that he generally said the same thing each time. He always started with: "This is the most important match you will ever play for Ireland." The night before the first Test, sure enough Murphy's first words were: "This is the most important match you will ever play." We were just after eating dinner and the room was very warm because there were twenty-five of us. Murphy was talking away for about five minutes and just as he said: "Jesus Christ ye're wearing the Irish jersey and do you realise this is the most important f**king game you will ever play?" there was a massive snore. It was, of course, Willie Duggan. Murphy said: "F**k it. I'm not doing this." Then he stormed out.'

TUFF STUFF

Willie's Lions captain, Phil Bennett, loved Duggan's willingness to take on physical confrontation in the most intimidating of environments. Hence his joking description of Willie: 'A fuse deliberately seeking a match.'

ALL I NEED IS THE AIR THAT I BREATHE

Scottish referees, like their goalkeepers, sometimes get a bad press. A Scottish referee, who shall remain nameless, was making his international debut in Twickenham in an England–Ireland Five Nations fixture in the 1970s. Willie Duggan was having a fag in the Irish dressing room. The time had come to run onto the pitch, but Duggan had nowhere to put out his cigarette. He knew that if he ran out with the fag in his mouth the cameras would zoom in on him straight away. When the referee came in to tell the teams it was time to leave, the Irish number eight went over to him and said: 'Would you hold that for a second please?' The obliging referee said yes, but Duggan promptly ran out on the pitch – leaving the ref with no option but to hold onto the fag. The ref went out to face the glare of the cameras and the first sight the television audience had was of him holding a cigarette. Asked about the incident afterwards, the referee said: 'I've had a wonderful day – but this wasn't it.'

AH REF

Willie Duggan sometimes got into trouble with referees. He was always phlegmatic about it: 'I don't consider I was sent off. The referee invited me to leave the pitch and I accepted the invitation.'

STAMPER

Fergus Slattery has one memory which sums up his famous colleague.

'In 1983 some of the guys played in a match against the Western Province in South Africa. The match was played in mid-July. Typical of Willie, all he took with him on the trip was a small bag with his toothbrush and cigarettes. Willie was never too bothered about training at the best of times, but in the middle of the summer he was totally unfit. The game passed right by him. At one stage I saw him stamping on the ground. I went over to him and asked him what the hell he was doing. He answered: "Oh, I'm stamping that bloody snail which has been following me around since the match started."'

JOYRIDERS

A famous tourist on the 1974 Lions tour was Fergus Slattery. An auctioneer by profession, Slats was not sold many dummies on the field. A product of Blackrock College, he was capped over sixty times for Ireland as an openside wing forward (a world record for a flanker), between 1970 and 1984, scoring three international tries. The classic story told about Slattery goes back to an African trip. After a British Lions tour fixture in Rhodesia, there was a celebratory dinner organised. The then-Rhodesian Prime Minister Ian Smith arrived to make a speech. Shortly after, two Irish players, Dick Milliken and Slats, decided to return to their hotel. Having consumed beverages stronger than orange juice, they were feeling particularly adventurous. As they walked out they noticed that just outside the entrance to the club was a beautiful black Cadillac with tinted windows. They decided to borrow the car and go for a drive. After driving around for a few minutes, the partition behind the front seats slid across and the Prime Minister asked: 'Are you gentlemen looking for a job?'

KEYS TO THE CITY

A constant source of amusement on the tour was the Welsh prop Bobby Windsor.

In the golden age of amateurism the manager of the Lions was Alan Thomas. He tended to lose things, especially room keys. He had a phone in his room, but each player on the team was only allowed one phone call a week. Windsor spotted Alan's key and held onto it. Every evening he used it to sneak in to Alan's room and phone his wife. As the tour concluded and the team were leaving the hotel, Alan came into the foyer and addressed the entire squad in a crestfallen voice:

'I'm very disappointed. I have been handed a phone bill for a thousand rand. One of you guys has been using the phone every night behind my back. The Lions are supposed to be the cream of rugby, but one of you has let the side down. Sadly, the guy who did this is a countryman of my own. He's been ringing Pontypridd.'

At this point Bobby Windsor jumped up from his seat and started waving his fists menacingly as he said, 'Which of you bast**ds has been phoning my wife?'

REASONS TO BE CHEERFUL

Fergus Slattery once asked Austin Healey if he had Irish blood. Healey replied with passionate intensity: 'I'm half Irish, but I will never, ever play for you.'

Slatts replied: 'Thank God for that.'

PARTY ANIMALS

In June 1983, Slats went to Barcelona with the Wolfhounds to play an exhibition game against a French selection. The match was to be played at midday. The evening before the game, Fergus was looking for somebody to go out with him for a night on the town. Under the circumstances, nobody wanted to take up his invitation, knowing the tough conditions that would await them the next day, but eventually he recruited the replacement prop-forward. The next morning the two lads returned from their adventures as the French team were heading out to train. Fergus was not a bit fazed. On the bus to the game Phil Orr was taken ill and to the horror of the 'partying' sub he had to take his place. Slats played like a man inspired, but nobody had ever seen anyone suffer on the pitch like his partner.

BIG IN JAPAN

Even when he departed the Irish scene, the great Irish and Leinster prop Phil Orr still had time for a last hurrah on the international stage:

'After the inaugural World Cup I retired from international rugby, but later that year I was invited to play for a World XV in Japan as part of the All Blacks tour. They had Japanese players at hooker and scrum half, with not a word of English between them. These are the two most important positions on the field in terms of making the calls on the pitch and giving instructions. It made absolutely no sense to have non-English speakers in those key positions in a team of essentially English speakers. We learned the Japanese for "one", "three" and "five" and limited ourselves to three calls. To confuse the opposition, I came up with the idea of using Japanese brand names so that our call would be "Honda One" in Japanese, for example. Then it was brought to my attention that one of the Japanese players worked for Honda and didn't like the company name being used in this way. So that ended my master plan.

'We all knew the All Blacks were in a mean mood. They had defeated Japan 106–4 in the Test game. The mistake the Japanese made was scoring a try. If they hadn't the cheek to score a try I reckon the All Blacks would have let them off with a fifty points defeat. I can't remember much about the match except that we were murdered in the first half at tight head prop. All I could say by way of tactical insight at half-time was: "We're going to retreat carefully."'

AMAZING GRACE

When Tom Grace played rugby he had jet black hair and a Beatles haircut, so it came as an enormous shock to him when his hair went grey. He was up in Donegal before one of the international matches with his family. RTÉ were showing some footage of tries from previous seasons. When they started to show a few of Grace's his wife rushed out to call his son, Conor, who was six at the time, to see his Dad in his prime. When Conor came in she pointed to the television excitedly and showed Grace in full flight. Conor just shook his head and said. 'No, it's not him. My dad has grey hair.' Then he just turned on his heels and ran out to play soccer.

SUDS

One of the captains of the UCD side Grace played on was Peter Sutherland, who became a giant in the business and economic world after he became European Commissioner in the 1980s. 'Suds' put his own stamp on the captaincy. The night before the Cup matches the UCD players met in his house in Monkstown. A walk on Dun Laoghaire pier became part of the ritual. For the first match they had sandwiches, tea, coffee and light drinks. As their Cup run progressed the refreshments became ever more lavish.

The night before the semi-final they had a totally fabulous dinner with all kinds of delicacies. Then Suds gave his speech. The food was incredibly memorable – the speech wasn't. The next day UCD lost narrowly … 28–3!

SHORT-CHANGED

Tom Grace was succeeded as Irish captain by his clubmate Johnny Moloney. Johnny was a very single-minded player. In a schoolboy match he was charging through for a try when a despairing dive by his marker robbed him of his shorts. True to form, he raced through for the try in his underpants before worrying about getting new togs.

SUPERSTITIOUS MINDS

Ireland's tour of Australia in 1979 provided one particularly amusing memory for Johnny Moloney:

'I was sharing a room with Terry Kennedy at one stage. Rodney O'Donnell was rooming with Mike Gibson. I can't think of a greater contrast of personalities, unless you put Tony O'Reilly rooming with Moss Keane. Mike was very dedicated, prepared meticulously and normally went to bed by ten. Rodney was very laid-back and an early night for him would be midnight. He went to Australia as a twenty-two-year-old St Mary's full back, an uncapped unknown, and returned as a hero.

'Rodney's middle name could have been Superstition. He had a huge fear of anything connected with the number thirteen. On tour not alone did he refuse to stay in a room numbered thirteen, or 213, or a room on the thirteenth floor, but he would not even stay in a room in which the numbers added up to thirteen like 274.

'When he believed in something there could be no deviation. He always insisted on being the last man on the team bus, and would patiently wait for everyone to assemble onto the bus regardless of the climatic conditions. He refused to walk over a line. On a stone pavement he would make the most bizarre movements to avoid treading on a line. With all this practice some of his fellow players said he could have been world champion at hopscotch.

'A Friday the thirteenth fell on the Lions tour in 1980. Ollie Campbell and John Robbie rose at 6.30 a.m. that morning and, with taping, made lines right across the lobby outside O'Donnell's room, and pasted the number thirteen all over the lobby and the elevator. As a result, Rodney was afraid to leave the room for the entire day.

'He had an interesting theory about the psychology of the rugby ball. When an opponent had kicked a goal against his team, he felt much better if the ball came down in such a way that he was able to throw it back over the crossbar, his theory being that the next time the ball was either unsure where to go, or would lose the habit of travelling in the right direction.

'Yet another ritual was preparing to tog out before games. He had to put on his togs in such a way that the material did not touch his skin on the way up. Should such a calamity occur he would begin the whole process again – and if necessary again and again until he got it exactly right. The second part of this operation was that he would never button up his togs until he was running onto the field.

'He was preoccupied with exactitudes to the point that he went around every room adjusting pictures so that they hung straight on the walls. This tendency was dramatically illustrated on Ireland's tour to Australia in 1979. In the middle of Noel Murphy's team talk he jumped up to the astonishment of all present to adjust the position of the telephone.

'One of his most famous idiosyncrasies was his desire to get into bed each night without touching the bottom sheet. The task had to be executed with military-like precision. If he failed the first time, he would repeat the process until he got it exactly right. Only then did he allow himself to relax.

'Rodney dropped into our room for a chat one night on that Australian tour and later we were joined by Paul McNaughton. Paul asked Rodney who he was rooming with. When he answered him Paul pretended to be very sympathetic, which made Rodney a tiny bit uncomfortable because Paul had shared with Gibo the week before. He told him that when he went back into the room he would discover that the sheets and blankets on his bed would be folded neatly, half way back, the light would be left on in the bathroom and the bathroom door would be left slightly ajar. Then when he went into bed, he would be asleep about half an hour when Gibo would jump on top of him in the bed. Rodney was very sceptical, but a couple of hours later when he went back to his room and saw it was just as Paul described: the light on in the toilet, the bathroom door slightly ajar and the covers folded back on the bed. The next morning he came down for his breakfast like a zombie. He told us he hadn't slept a wink all night because he was waiting for Gibo to jump on top of him.'

JOHNNY-COME-LATELY

Johnny Moloney also toured with the Lions in South Africa in 1974. Near the end of the tour he was summonsed before the players' informal court. Johnny was charged with a very serious offence – he hadn't 'enjoyed conjugal relations' with any woman on the tour, even though he was still single at the time. In his defence Johnny said, very unconvincingly, that he had in fact slept with two women. Tom Grace said immediately, 'Shagger'.

Shortly after they returned, Mick Quinn saw Johnny at a reception with his girlfriend, later his wife, Miriam and he shouted over at him, 'How's it going, Shagger?' Miriam discreetly asked Quinn why he had called him Shagger. Quinn told her that what goes on a tour is sacred and there was no way he could disclose any intimate details about Johnny's behaviour. Moloney had some explaining to do that night.

CALL GIRL

One figure looms large in Moloney's comic reminiscences of his days with Ireland:

'We were playing England away. Stewart McKinney went through the pages of *Mayfair* magazine and saw the number of an escort service. He rang it up and booked a lady of the night for Mick Quinn. I had to play my part by keeping Quinny in his room and slipping out just before she was due to arrive. I only know this from hearsay, you understand, but she was wearing a raincoat with nothing on underneath but suspenders and some very skimpy underwear. Quinny had to pay her £25 just to get her out of the room. After she left he came out the corridor and everyone in the squad was looking out from their rooms laughing at him. It was the only time I ever saw him lost for words.'

NO ORDINARY JOE

In conversation with this writer, Irish coach Joe Schmidt revealed the two biggest hazards of being Irish rugby coach: 'One is injuries and the other is that Mick Quinn is always taking the p*** out of me.'

SUPERQUINN

'Mine has been an eventful career.' This is Mick Quinn's summation of his life in rugby which brought him ten caps for Ireland as out-half:

'I enjoyed every minute of my international career. I don't think I ever played a bad game for Ireland, which is a good feeling to have. The great thing about rugby is the friendship, even with your rivals for the Irish jersey. I get on great with Tony Ward even though he was the main impediment to my international career. In his biography, *The Good, The Bad and The Rugby*, Tony jokes that if it wasn't for Ollie Campbell he would have got forty caps. When I read that I rang him up and said if it wasn't for him, Mike Gibson, Barry McGann, Ollie and Paul Dean I would have won eighty caps.'

For his part, Barry McGann jokes: 'I got Mick Quinn his ten caps for Ireland because I was his only competition and I wasn't up to much at the time.'

AGAINST THE HEAD

One of Quinn's most endearing qualities is being able to tell stories against himself.

'After one international match a young autograph hunter said to me: "Can I have your autograph please, Johnny?" I didn't have the heart to tell him he had got the wrong man so I just signed it. "To Bert. Best wishes, Johnny Moloney." As he was leaving he looked up and said to me: "How do you keep playing with Mick Quinn. He plays like sh*t."'

COMPETITION

Quinn relished his rivalry with both Ward and Campbell.

'Wardy's great champion was Ned van Esbeck of *The Irish Times*. Whenever I kicked a great penalty it was just a great penalty, but when Wardy kicked one it was "a wonder strike from the master craftsman". Whenever I was kicking exceptionally well I would shout up at Ned and ask him whether or not Wardy could have bettered that.

'There was a time I got one up on Ollie. I am good friends with Chris de Burgh, and was with him in Rome for the World Cup quarter-final in 1990 when Ireland lost to Italy. It was incredible to see the way all the Italians mobbed Chris before the game, but we went into the middle of the crowd just as ordinary fans. I saw some of the U2 guys up in the stands with their bodyguards away from the riff-raff, but Chris wasn't like that. After the match Jack Charlton and the players went on the team bus, but the Irish fans were still in the stadium yelling for Jack. I ran out and asked him to come back out on the pitch which he did. I walked out behind him and when I looked up there was Ollie in the stands. So I waved at him knowing full well he would be wondering to himself how that so-and-so Quinn managed to get on the pitch with Jack Charlton.'

BARE NECESSITIES

Quinn's career brought some revealing moments:

'One of the highlights of my career was winning the three-in-a-row of Leinster Cups in 1981 with Lansdowne. We beat Old Belvedere in the final and it was nice to put one over on Ollie on the pitch. After the match the team bus was bringing us on to the victory celebrations. I suggested to the boys we should "lob a moon", or display our bums, out the window to the people of Dublin. This proposal was enthusiastically agreed to. When we were on display I turned around and saw there was a car travelling alongside the bus. To my horror, the occupants were my father, mother and sister. My mother told me afterwards that she had recognised my bum because it hadn't changed since the time she used to change my nappies. I told her I found that hard to believe.'

DOZY

Quinn's rise to the top was meteoric:

'After I left school I joined Lansdowne. In my first year I played for the third team. The next season I was on the first team and playing for Ireland when I was only twenty. I don't remember much about the build-up for my debut except that I fell asleep during Willie John McBride's team talk. Ray McLoughlin told me that I was a cheeky bugger.'

NUMBER ONE

Quinn's first international was memorable. 'It was pay for play with a difference. I had to pay for my jersey. We beat France 6–4 for my first cap. The player who scored their try was killed by lightning some time later. The great J.P. Romeu missed the conversion. As it was my first cap there was no way I was going to part with my jersey, but I really wanted Romeu's. I went back into the dressing room and asked Ray McLoughlin for his number one jersey. You have to remember that he is a very successful businessman, who headed up the James Crean Company, so he's not short of a few bob. He sold me his jersey for £10. I rushed out and swapped jerseys with Romeu. I was thrilled with myself when I returned but suddenly the French man came into our dressing room. With his dreadful English, and my awful French, communication was a problem but it didn't take me long to see that the problem was that he wanted a number ten jersey. I used sign language and said to him: "Zero fello offo."'

RAY OF SUNSHINE

Quinn had a great affection for the late Ray Gravell:

'Ray, like a lot of the Welsh players, was really nationalistic. Once before an international, when I was sub, I went into the toilet and I heard Ray in the next cubicle singing arias about the welcome in the hills in Wales. I told him that the only reason they welcomed us in the hills was that they were too mean to invite us into their homes.

There's a limit to the amount of Ray's singing I can take so I asked him to give it a rest, but he went on and on. To shut him up I filled a bucket of cold water and threw it over him in the cubicle. I fled because he came out like a raging bull and I said nothing about the incident in our dressing room. When the Welsh team came out some of our lads remarked that Ray must have gone through an awfully heavy warm-up because the sweat was rolling off him.'

FRIENDS FROM FAR AWAY

Through his involvement with the Wolfhounds Quinn continued to have plenty of contact with the giants of international rugby:

'I met J. P. R. Williams one day at the end of 1990. It was the time Wales had gone thirteen international matches without winning. He's always beating the nationalist drum, going on about the rugby in the valleys in Wales and how central it is to Welsh life. It was nice, in a way, to see him eating humble pie so I asked him what his most fervent wish for Welsh rugby in 1991 was. He answered: "I hope that Wales win a match." He then asked me what my most fervent wish for Irish rugby was for that year. I said: "For Ireland to win the Triple Crown, the Grand Slam and the World Cup." He said: "Ah, come on Mick, be serious." All I said to him was: "You f**king started it."

'The former English international Gareth Chilcott earns a fortune from making speeches. I once played a golf match with him during the Lions tour of New Zealand. At one stage my ball trickled into a pond. I could see it and asked him to hold my hand as I leaned over to retrieve it. He said he would, but deliberately let me go and I toppled in. I had to take off all my clothes and try and squeeze the water out of them, much to the bemusement of the women who were playing on the other greens.'

WITH A LITTLE HELP FROM MY FRIENDS

Quinn developed a closer friendship than he envisaged with a legend of South African rugby:

'At one stage Willie John McBride and I were invited there to play for a World XV against the Springboks. I was interviewed on South African TV and asked if any of the South African out-halves had impressed me. I mentioned that I had been taken by this new kid called Naas Botha who I had seen play on television. The next day I was training when this fella came over to me and I recognised him as Botha. He wanted to thank me for my compliments.

'Naas was a hugely controversial figure in South Africa. They either loved him or hated him. We got on very well, and I subsequently invited him to come over and get some experience in Lansdowne. I thought nothing more about it until some months later I got a phone call at home. It was Naas. He said he would like to take up my offer of hospitality. I told him that he would be welcome and asked him when he would be travelling over. Then he told me: "Well Mr Quinn, I'm ringing you from a place called O'Connell Street in Dublin." He brought his brother, Darius, with him, who since became a Dutch Reformed Minister. He used to organise prayer meetings in my house.'

HOW NOT TO MAKE FRIENDS

While Quinn's gregarious personality has won him many friends in rugby, it has not always helped his career to advance.

'In general I have great memories of playing with Leinster. One of the people I played with was Brian O'Driscoll's dad, Frank. Like Brian he was a great tackler. I played my final match for Leinster in the Sportsground in Galway in 1984 when we were going for the Championship. It was an awful day with the wind and the rain, which made it impossible for me to run the ball. There was only a handful of people in the stand, one of whom was Mick "the

Cud" Cuddy, the former Ireland and Leinster selector. The only thing I could hear was a constant chorus from "the Cud" of "Run the bloody ball, Leinster." I got so fed up I shouted up at him: "Cuddy, shut your f**kin' mouth." He was furious and roared down at me: "That's the last time you'll play for Leinster."'

BORING

Quinn enjoys the humour in other sports:

'One player I always admired was Manchester United's Denis Irwin. I attended Irwin's testimonial dinner. Jack Charlton brought the house down there with his unconventional tribute to Denis. Jack said, "Denis was the consummate professional; the best full back to play for Manchester United; the best full back to play for the Republic of Ireland. He was always our most consistent player; he never made mistakes; he never gave the ball away; he was always on time for training; always first on the bus for training; he never let you down nor never once caused a problem. What a boring, f**king bast**d."'

GRIZZLY ALEX

They don't come much tougher than Alex 'Grizz' Wyllie. The former All Blacks coach was not a man to mess with on the pitch, as Ireland's fly-half Mick Quinn discovered to his detriment on Ireland's New Zealand tour in 1976. Ireland were losing 15–3 to Canterbury. Quinn was sub. From his point of view everything was going great. When you are a sub you don't really want things to be going well for the team because if it does how else are you going to get your place back? Full back Larry Moloney broke his arm so Tony Ensor replaced him. Then Wallace McMaster got injured and with a sinking in his heart Quinn realised he would have to play on the wing. It was his first time ever playing in that position. He was petrified.

As he walked on 'Grizz' Wyllie came over to him and said: 'You've come a long way to die son.' When Quinn was in school his coach had always drilled in to him the belief that he should never let anybody intimidate him. At that stage he made the biggest mistake of his life. He said to Wyllie: 'Listen pal if my dog had a face like yours I would shave his arse and get him to walk backwards.' Every chance Wyllie got after that he clobbered Quinn. Even when the ball was somewhere else he kept coming at Quinn. When the Irish man said the ball is over there Wyllie answered: 'I couldn't give a f**k where the ball is. I'm going to kill you.'

NICKNAMES

Perhaps Quinn's most enduring legacy to the rugby landscape is the number of players he has given nicknames to.

'I called former international scrum half Tony Doyle "Gandhi" because there was more meat in a cheese sandwich. I called the Wesley player Dave Priestman "Vicarman" because I told him it was ridiculous for a Protestant to be called priest. I call Brendan Mullin "Bugs Bunny" because of his smile. I also christened Harry Steele "Stainless" for obvious reasons and Jean Pierre Rives – now a noted sculptor, and the living proof that you don't have to be big to be a world-class forward – "*Je t'aime*" because he had such charm with women. I called my Lansdowne clubmate Rory Moroney "the Reverend Moroney" because he spent two years in the priesthood.'

MURPHY'S LAW

Quinn has great affection for his former playing colleagues. One former Irish international he recalls as much for his off the field activities as for his playing career.

'Johnny Murphy was a great captain for Leinster. He has a bus and hearse business and turned up for training one night in his hearse with a coffin inside. Some of the Leinster players found it disconcerting to be doing their press-ups beside a coffin and grumbled to Johnny. He just said, "She's not going anywhere and doesn't mind waiting."

'Johnny's speeches were memorable not least because he was great at taking off posh accents. His opening sentence after a Connacht match was, "Mr President of Leinster, Mr President of Connacht, players and the rest of you hangers on." He made more politically incorrect remarks and was told by the "blazers" to tone down his speeches. The next week Leinster played Llanelli and beat the pants off them. Everyone was dying to know what Johnny would say. He began, "Well lads I've got to be very careful what I say this week. It was a great honour for us to have the privilege of playing against such a famous side. My only regret is that BBC's *Rugby Special* wasn't here to see us beating the sh*te out of ye. I know people will say ye were missing some of your star players but don't forget we were missing one of our greatest stars – Hugo MacNeill. He couldn't get his f**king place – I have it." The whole place was in stitches and Ray Gravell in particular had to be picked off the floor he was laughing so hard.'

THE YOUNG ONES

Ollie Campbell would probably be seen as the crown prince of his generation of Irish rugby. Mick Quinn is more likely to be seen as the clown prince. Yet he has a serious side:

'I would like to think I have an eye for a young player of promise. The first time I saw John Robbie play was when he played for The High School. I went over to him after the match and said: "You'll play for Ireland."

Years later I won £100 for him. I was playing a club match and there was a guy slagging me all through the match, saying I was useless. We got a penalty fifteen yards inside our half and ten yards in from the touchline. I had the wind behind me and John bet a pound at a hundred to one that I would score and I did.'

University Challenge

Robbie went on to study at Cambridge University where he was elected skipper of the rugby team ahead of Eddie Butler, who was destined to become one of the legends of Welsh rugby. Robbie was a bit taken aback by the side's preparation for the glamour fixture against Oxford. A few days before the big name they had a nuts and port dinner and toasted Oxford in the traditional way. They stood and said G.D.B.O. – God Damn Bloody Oxford. He scored seventeen points in the game, including a spectacular try. He jokes that his one regret was that he missed out on Alastair Hignell's record for a varsity game. He had instructed the team to run a penalty from in front of the posts at one stage, but had he known he was just two off the record he would have kicked it.

Laughter is the Best Medicine

Robbie retains many funny memories from his time with the Lions in 1979:

'At one stage I went fishing with Ollie Campbell in Durban. Ollie got as sick as a dog and was hurling his guts overboard. He also got caught a whopper of a fish, a Barracuda. As he was feeling so ill he asked one of the crew to help him row in the fish. He was promptly told: "The rule of this boat is that you pull in your own fish." At the best of times Ollie looks pale, but that day he looked whiter than a sheet.

'At one stage, quite near the end, we were all called into a special meeting. Syd Millar addressed us and asked if we were unhappy, as he had read reports to that effect. We all said we were having a whale of time. He then asked us if we would all return to tour South Africa if selected. I was the only player who indicated that I would have to think about it; everyone else said they would. In fact Peter Morgan, the young Welsh utility player who had played in only a few games on the tour, brought the house down by saying that he'd love to come back again as next time they might let him have a game.'

TOURING

After the tour Robbie decided to stay on in South Africa and further his rugby career there:

'When I moved to South Africa I discovered that one of the benefits of being a high profile sportsman in South Africa was sponsorship. I was given a car around the same time I was dropped by Transvaal. The panel on the door read: "Opel supports John Robbie." Some wit suggested that the lower panel should read: "Transvaal doesn't".'

HOMEWARD BOUND

On his rare trips back to Ireland Robbie enjoys the opportunity of seeing the Irish team play. He doesn't always get the reception he expects:

'I left Ireland in 1981 after we were whitewashed. In '82 Ireland won the Triple Crown and in '83 the Championship. I timed my first trip home to Ireland in '84 to coincide with Ireland's Five Nations game against Wales. Ireland were whitewashed again that season. I had missed out on two glorious years for Ireland and came home to see them losing again, an experience I was all too familiar with from my playing days. After the Welsh game I was still in the stand as the crowd was thinning. I heard a voice shouting, "Robbie, Robbie". I looked around until I found the owner of this voice. When I eventually met this stranger's eye he said: "John Robbie, I'm addressing you." I was very flattered to be recognised and gave him the royal wave. After all the drama though he took the wind out of my sails when he said: "You're some f**king good luck charm."'

THE BLACK MARKET

Top Irish club, St Mary's, toured Russia in 1977. It was a strange environment at the time because they had two Russian police going everywhere with them, keeping tabs on everything they did. It was the pre-Glasnost, pre-Perestroika era, and everybody in Russia was mad for Western goods, especially jeans. They had all their team blazers and jumpers and O'Neills playing gear so they were able to sell off their jeans for about €100 in today's money. But their masterstroke was to convince the Russians that O'Neills was the Irish for Adidas. That tour cost the players virtually nothing as a result of their black market activities.

VERBAL LYNCH MOB

In 1971 Colin Meads prematurely dismissed the Lions forwards as, 'Too many sweat bands, not enough sweat.' Seán Lynch was one of the men who made Meads eat his words. Capped seventeen times for his country, Lynch is not a player to take himself too seriously. Lynchie was on the Irish tour to Argentina in 1970. All the players were attending a dinner. A 'Lord somebody' was to be the main dignitary. Before he arrived, the players were told that he had Parkinson's disease and to be patient as it would take him a long time to walk to the dinner table. So it transpired as the Lord slowly made his way to the seating position. He was sitting beside Lynchie and said, 'Well Mr Lynch are you enjoying your tour?' Lynchie replied, 'Yes, Mr Parkinson, I am.'

COLOURFUL

Lynch was one of the surprise stars of the Lions tour in 1971. He was to play a more central role than anybody could have foreseen at the start of the tour. The week before the first Test in Dunedin the Lions had lost their two first choice props, Ray McLoughlin and Sandy Carmichael, who sustained long-term injuries in the infamous 'battle of Christchurch'. The match confirmed an old adage: 'New Zealand rugby is a colourful game – you get all black and blue.'

The Life of O'Reilly

There are two types of people in the world: those who make things happen and those that things happen to. Tony O'Reilly was probably in both camps.

Rugby players sometimes suffer from 'Orson Welles syndrome'. Like the famous star of the screen, their crowning moment of glory came at the very start of their careers. Nothing that followed could match it.

Tony O'Reilly became a rugby superstar on the Lions tour to South Africa in 1955, even though he was still a teenage novice at international rugby. He is very much the 'Roy of the Rovers' of Irish rugby. Having been capped against France as an eighteen-year-old in 1955, he really made his mark with the Lions.

O'Reilly celebrated his nineteenth birthday on the Lions tour to South Africa in 1955. In the opening Test the Lions won 23–22 in Johannesburg. It was the biggest attendance ever seen at a rugby game. The Springboks led 11–3, and to compound their misfortune the Lions lost their flanker Reg Higgins to a broken leg. At the time no replacements were allowed, so they had to play with fourteen men in front of over 100,000 partisan South Africans. Then three tries from Cliff Morgan, Cecil Pedlow and Tony O'Reilly gave the Lions a 23–11 lead. The Afrikaners replied with a vengeance. In the final minute Chris Koch crashed over for a try to cut the deficit to just one point. As van der Schyff faced a relatively easy kick to give the South Africans victory, the Irish members on the team turned to religion. The Limerick second row Tom Reid said, 'Jesus, if he kicks this I'm turning Protestant.'

To the horror of the home fans, van der Schyff pushed his kick left of the post.

O'Reilly's quick wit was evident. Asked as to what he had been doing looking the other way as Springbok goal-kicking ace van der Schyff took the kick which would have given South Africa victory, he replied: 'I was in direct communion with the Vatican.' Van der Schyff missed and the tourists won 23–22.

From sight to insight

The late Tom Reid was a great diplomat, and saw rugby as a 'little refreshment of my spirit'. On the tour, O'Reilly and Reid were amongst a group of Lions tourists who were asked about their views of the political situation during an official reception on the tour. An awkward silence descended on the party until Reid piped up, 'Well, sir, I think nothing of it. I come from Limerick in southern Ireland and I have my own political problems.'

Reid suffered from bad eyesight and went to live in Canada after that tour. In 1959 he memorably linked up with O'Reilly again. After that year's tour in New Zealand the Lions stopped off to play a Test in Canada. O'Reilly was standing in line before the match when he heard a loud Limerick accent booming out over the ground, 'Hello Reilly, I know you're there. I can't see you but I can hear you all right.'

Rough play

As a schoolboy O'Reilly also excelled at soccer, playing for Home Farm, but he turned his back on the game on foot of an assault. During a match he made a bone-crunching tackle on an opponent. The boy's mother rushed onto the pitch and attacked O'Reilly with her umbrella. The future Lions sensation remarked: 'Rugby is fair enough – you only have your opponent to deal with. Soccer you can keep, if it involves having to deal with your opponent and his mother.'

Business school

Belvedere College provided a nursery for both O'Reilly's rugby and entrepreneurial skills. When he was seven he was the only boy in his class to make Holy Communion. To mark the occasion a priest gave him an orange – an enormous luxury during the war years. Like most of his friends, O'Reilly had never seen an orange.

O'Reilly subsequently claimed: 'After I ate the centre I sold the peel for one penny per piece, thereby showing a propensity for commercial deception which has not left me since.'

TACTICAL AWARENESS

In 1963, following Ireland's 24–5 defeat at the hands of the French, O'Reilly was dropped for the only time in his career. Although the news came as a shock, O'Reilly had arguably never consistently reproduced his Lions form in the green jersey. It seemed that after twenty-eight caps his international career was over. Seven years later, in an ill-judged move, the Irish selectors persuaded him to come out of retirement to play against England at Twickenham in place of the injured Billy Brown for his twentieth-ninth cap. To put it at its kindest, O'Reilly, now firmly established as a commercial giant because of his work with the Heinz corporation, was anything but a lean, mean machine at that time. His shape prompted Willie John McBride to remark: 'Well, Tony, in my view your best attacking move tomorrow might be to shake your jowls at them.'

Ireland lost 9–3, and O'Reilly gave an undistinguished performance. In the final moments he dived boldly into the heart of the English pack. As he regained consciousness he heard an Irish voice shouting: 'And while you're at it, why don't ya kick his f**king chauffeur too.'

The Heinz slogan is: 'Beanz Means Heinz.' After the match a wag was heard to say: 'I never realised Heinz means has-beens.'

ISLANDS IN THE STREAM

Sir Anthony was once urged by the great Irish flank forward Ronnie Kavanagh to harden himself with a gruelling physical regime in the mountains. O'Reilly was typically unimpressed: 'Kav, it's not guerilla warfare, it's rugby we're playing. We're not going to be asked to ford a stream at Lansdowne Road.'

WORD PERFECT

There are good public speakers, there are great public speakers and there's Tony O'Reilly.

After listening to O'Reilly give a lengthy speech in his alma mater, Taoiseach Bertie Ahern said: 'I'd like to congratulate Belvedere College on the great job they did in teaching Tony O'Reilly to speak so well. A pity they didn't teach him to stop.'

HUSBANDS AND WIVES

O'Reilly is one of the greatest raconteurs world rugby has ever produced. When Éamon de Valera was in his final few years as Irish president he was virtually blind, but he was persuaded to attend one of Ireland's home internationals. Watching the game in the stands, Tony O'Reilly was unhappy with some of the referee's decisions. When he was asked afterwards to comment on the match he said: 'Dev saw more of it than the referee.'

O'Reilly once told the story of an unnamed Irish international whose wife arrived home from work early one day and found her husband in bed with another woman. 'That's it,' she shouted, 'I'm leaving and I'm not coming back!'

'Wait honey,' the Irish international pleaded, 'Can't you at least let me explain?'

'Fine, let's hear your story,' the wife replied.

'Well, I was driving home when I saw this poor young lady sitting at the side of the road, barefoot, torn clothes, covered in mud and sobbing. I immediately took pity on her and asked if she would like to get cleaned up. She got into the car and I brought her home. After she took a shower, I gave her a pair of the underwear that doesn't fit you anymore, the dress that I bought you last year that you never wore, the pair of shoes you bought but never used and even gave her some of the turkey you had in the refrigerator but didn't serve me. Then I showed her to the door and she thanked me. As she was walking down the step, she turned around and asked me, 'Is there anything else your wife doesn't use anymore?'

Another of the stories attributed to O'Reilly was about the Irish international who was having an affair with an Italian woman. One night she confided in him that she was pregnant. Not wanting to ruin his reputation or his marriage, he paid her a large sum of money if she would go to Italy to have the child. If she stayed in Italy, he would also provide child support until the child turned eighteen. She agreed, but wondered how he would know when the baby was born. To keep it discreet, he told her to send him a postcard, and write 'Spaghetti' on the back. He would then arrange for child support. One day, almost nine months later, he came home to his confused wife, Martina. 'Darling,' she said, 'you received a very strange postcard today.'

'Oh, just give it to me and I'll explain it later,' he said.

Martina obeyed, and watched as the Irish international read the card, turned white and fainted.

On the card was written, 'Spaghetti, Spaghetti, Spaghetti. Two with meatballs, one without.'

MEMENTO

Cliff Morgan was one of the great Welsh number tens. In 1952 he scored a stunning try to win the Triple Crown for Wales against Ireland in Lansdowne Road. His proud father was so thrilled that he leapt to his feet and shouted with joy, spitting out his false teeth twenty rows in front of him – never to see them again. When he recalled that story on RTÉ television with Tony O'Reilly, the Irish man quipped: 'I know a farmer from Limerick who is still wearing them.'

IT SAYS IN THE PAPERS

The late Irish flanker Jim McCarthy was best man at both of O'Reilly's weddings, though he only played the one season with Tony at international level. When he arrived on the scene he was the darling of the media and could do no wrong. After his first match against France *The Irish Independent* said that Jim had played poorly and had not protected Tony well enough, even though he wasn't playing in the centre. He was dropped for the next match after that report and never played another international. Twenty-five years later, when O'Reilly had become the owner of the paper Tony put him on the board of *The Irish Independent* just to make up for their injustice to him all those years ago.

LADIES MAN

A gentleman to his fingertips, Jim would not reveal Tony O'Reilly's roommate from the night before Ireland played against England at Twickenham. O'Reilly was out having a good time and his bored roommate was sitting in the room alone when the phone rang. A young woman's voice came over the line. 'Can I speak to Tony please?'

'I'm sorry, he's not in right now. Can I take a message?'

'Do you know what time he'll be back?'

'I think he said he'd be home around ten.'

Silence. Awkward silence.

'Do you want to leave a message for Tony? I'd be happy to pass it on to him as soon as he comes in.'

'Well … he said he would be in at this time and asked me to call him.'

'Well, he went out with Karen about an hour ago and said he would be back at ten.'

A shocked voice now: 'Who the fu … who is Karen?'

'The girl he went out with.'

'I know that. I mean … who is she?'

'I don't know her last name. Look, do you want to leave a message for Tony?'

'Yes … please do. Tell him to call me when he gets in.'

'I sure will. Is this Mary-Kate?'

'Who the f**king hell is Mary-Kate?'

'Well, he's going out with Mary-Kate at ten. I thought you were her. Sorry. It was an honest mistake.'

'Tony's the one that made the mistake. Tell him that Liz called and that's she's very upset and that I would like him to call me as soon as he gets in.'

'Okay, I will … but Samantha isn't going to like this.'

The phone was slammed down with venom.

AND AS FOR FORTUNE AND AS FOR FAME

McCarthy believed that tours are rugby's tales of the unexpected. One episode which proves the accuracy of that remark came in 1952 when Ireland toured South America. It was a total success off the field and a disaster on it. They were the first international team to be beaten by Argentina. When the Irish team got there they were told they couldn't play any rugby because Eva Perón had just died. They sent the boys in green down to Santiago, Chile to teach the cadets how to play. After eight days, the cadets beat the Irish.

The players didn't take the playing side very seriously. At one stage Paddy Lawler went missing for a few days and nobody had a clue where he was. When he returned, a team meeting was hastily called. The team manager solemnly announced that he had been talking to Dublin, which was a big deal in 1952, and then looked around menacingly and said, 'I'm deciding whether or not to send some players home.' Paddy stood up straight away and replied, 'We've been talking amongst ourselves and we're deciding whether or not we should send you home.'

LITTLE AND LARGE

Des O'Brien went on to become Irish captain after that tour. Before an international the then President of Ireland, Seán T. O'Kelly, the first Irish president to attend a rugby international, was being introduced to the teams. He was a man who was, let's say, small in stature. The match was being played in October so the grass was long. As captain, Des was introduced to him first. He said, 'God Bless you Des. I hope you have a good game.' Then O'Brien heard a booming voice in the crowd, 'Hey Des, would you ever get the grass cut so we'd bloody well be able to see the president.'

KEEPING UP WITH THE JONES BOY

Des was not the sort of man for histrionics. So when he managed the Lions team on the 1966 tour he did not panic when the Welsh centre Ken Jones went up the mountains to shoot deer with some local men, even though he got no permission from anyone to do so. When Jones was missing for a few days Des chose to ignore those who suggested he call the police, assuring them that Jones would be fine. The night before the next match was due, Jones coolly strolled into the restaurant where the team were having their dinner. Des never blinked and gently asked: 'Nice to see you, Ken. Tell me, will you be joining us for the game tomorrow?'

THAT'LL CLINCH IT

In the 1920s, one of the great characters of Irish rugby was Dr Jamie Clinch. When he was a medical student in Trinity College, Dublin he was sitting on the rail outside when an American tourist emerged from her first visit to the College and spoke to him. 'It's a big place, I've been three hours going through it,' she said. Jamie replied, 'Ma'am, I've been here for seven years and I'm not through it yet.'

In his medical examination Clinch was shown a bone and was asked what it was.

'A femur,' he replied.

'Right or left?'

'I'm not doing Honours,' he answered.

THE SPY WHO CAME IN FROM THE COLD

Possibly one of the most famous 'back room' characters in Irish rugby was UCD and Leinster's Ned Thornton. One of the stories told about Ned is about the day that he went to General Costello's funeral. There was a huge crowd outside as well as inside the church. The carriage came out with the coffin draped in the tricolour, with a hat and a stick on it. The troops sounded the death march and everybody was very solemn. Ned was standing beside Blackrock's Dan McCarthy at the time and turned around to him and said: 'I see he only got the one cap.'

CHAPTER FIVE

Observe the Sons of Ulster Marching On

There are moments of grace in every life when you cross paths with someone truly extraordinary. For me, meeting Jack Kyle was one of those special moments. The game needs characters, and Jack was one of them. He was also a strong personality, and such an intelligent analyst of the game. Sadly Jack left us as this book was being written after eighty-eight years of an amazing life. I will smile for all the great memories I have of him rather than cry for the national treasure we have lost. He left me a rich literary legacy. Like Joe Schmidt, he corresponded with the most beautiful handwritten letters.

Former world boxing champion Chris Eubank tried to stop his son playing rugby because it is 'the most vicious sport on God's earth'. This is to fundamentally misunderstand the sport and to almost criminally fail to appreciate its innate aesthetic appeal. Jack Kyle showed that rugby really is the beautiful game.

After Jack's death was announced, Irish fans filled the bars of Ireland with nostalgia. The post-mortems were not the most objective the rugby world has ever heard. The experts catalogued his achievement in a long line of great Irish heroes, warriors and miscellaneous feats of Celtic courage. No metaphor was too layered in hyperbole, particularly as the drink took effect. Strong men came dangerously close to blubbering. A few got so emotional that they did the unthinkable – they hugged without embarrassment.

Memory is softened by time. Rugby needs every nostalgic prop it can get, and all that Kyle exerted on the popular imagination will be his legacy. This chapter celebrates Jack and the legends of Ulster rugby.

MEDICAL SERVICE

Jack was one of the greats; not just of Irish rugby, but of international rugby. However, his father knew how to put him in his place: 'When my late father read that I had been selected to head off on a six month tour with the Lions, his words across the breakfast table were: "Does that young fellow ever intend to qualify in medicine?"'

Did the players receive any reward for their unique achievement in winning the Grand Slam in 1948?

'The only thing we got was a photo of the winning team and the team crest.'

That day's highly programmed game, which was dominated by patterns, was totally alien to Kyle:

'In all my time playing for Ireland, planned tactics never came into it. I must have partnered eight or nine scrum halves in my time, and we'd just run out saying "Let's do our best and see how it goes."'

TACTICAL INNOVATION

Jack witnessed some strange sights at team meetings:

'I remember my former teammate Andy Mulligan telling the story of an Irish team talk given by my late brother-in-law, Noel Henderson, when he was captain of Ireland: "Right, lads, let's decide how we're going to play this game. What do you think, Jack?"

'I responded, "A few wee punts at the line might be dandy, and maybe young Mulligan here can try a few darts of his own."

'Noel then sought Tony O'Reilly's opinion. O'Reilly replied, "The programme here says a midget's marking me. Just give me the ball and let me have a run at him."

'Then it was Cecil Pedlow's turn. Cec's answer was, "I think a subtle mix of runnin', jinkin' an' kickin' should work out just fine."

'Picking up the ball to go out, Noel summed up: "Right, lads, that's decided – Jack's puntin', Andy's dartin', Tony's runnin', and Cecil's doin' all three."'

LOSING MY RELIGION

The only story ever told against Jack Kyle is that he could be a little bit absent-minded at times, as when he turned up at an Ireland training session with only one boot.

For his part, Kyle greatly enjoyed some of the characters on the Irish team. He had a particular appreciation for the quick wit of former Irish rugby international Andy Mulligan, who once went up from Dublin to Belfast for a job. His prospective boss asked him: What religion are you, Mulligan?'

Quick as a flash Andy responded, 'What religion did you have in mind, sir?'

JOY AND SADNESS

After his post-surgery retirement, Jack lived in a 'wee village' on the County Down coastline. He was a gentleman in every sense of the word, and placed a high value on friendship. One of his friends had always wanted to visit Paris and Jack brought him there for his ninetieth birthday. His friend was suitably impressed by the wonders of one of the great cities in the world. At one stage they were sitting by the Seine sipping coffee. During that time a large number of beautiful women passed by. Jack's friend turned to him and shook his head sadly: 'Ah Jack, if only I was seventy again.'

THE BARE ESSENTIALS

The past is a different country, and listening to Jack was like travelling in a time warp: 'We were really innocent. I suppose this was particularly shown when we went to Paris in 1948. We had our banquet in the Hotel Laetitia. It was a bit of an eye-opener. There were six different glasses, a different wine for every course, all vintage. I will never forget the wine waiter coming along to pour for some of the Irish lads and they telling him, *"Non, non merci, avez-vous un jus d'orange, s'il vous plait?"* After that, we headed to the *Folies Bergère*, or in the immortal words of Bill McKay, the Folies Bareskins. It came as a culture shock to be looking at women whose breasts were uncovered.

'Travelling to Paris for us at the time was like going to the edge of the world. We were as green as grass. After our win we were invited to a reception at the Irish embassy. Of course, champagne was the order of the day, which was a very novel experience for most of us. We were knocking it back as if it was stout. To me the incident that best illustrated our innocence was when the Dolphin pair, Jim McCarthy and Bertie O'Hanlon, asked for red lemonade.'

GRAND CENTRAL

Kyle had some peculiar experiences playing rugby in Ireland. Shortly after the Grand Slam triumph in 1948, Jack drove down to Cork. On the way he came to a level crossing at a railway station which was halfway across the road. He sat in the car for ten minutes and then got out and found the station master and asked, 'Do you know the gate is halfway across the road?'

'I do,' replied the stationmaster. 'We are half expecting the train from Cork.'

DOCTOR, DOCTOR

Jack told me a few stories about his time as a doctor. One of his colleagues, who was known for his extraordinary treatment of arthritis, had a waiting room full of people when a little old lady, bent over almost in half, shuffled in slowly, leaning on her cane. When her turn came, she went into the doctor's office. Within five minutes she came back out walking completely erect. A woman in the waiting room who had seen all this rushed up to the little old lady and said, 'It's a miracle. You walked in bent in half, and now you're walking erect. What did the doctor do?'

'Gave me a longer cane,' the woman replied.

GLORY DAYS

One of the giants of Irish rugby in the golden era of Jackie Kyle was his brother-in-law, Noel Henderson. In the course of a radio commentary of an Irish international, Henderson was being slated by the commentator. Noel's father was so outraged at the stream of insults that he threw the radio out the window.

HOPE AND HOPELESSNESS

Henderson's most famous declaration was, 'The state of British sport is mostly serious, but never hopeless. The state of Irish sport is usually hopeless, but never serious.'

I'LL DO ANYTHING FOR LOVE

One of Noel's teammates on the Grand Slam winning side was J. C. Daly. Jack was an extraordinary character, and one of rugby's great romantics. Before World War II he only played with the thirds for London Irish. As he departed for combat he said: 'When I come back I'll be picked for Ireland.' He was stationed in Italy during the war and had to carry heavy wireless equipment on his back. As a result, his upper body strength was incredible. Before internationals he did double somersaults to confirm his fitness.

Having scored the winning try to give Ireland the Grand Slam in 1948 he was nearly killed by spectators at the final whistle. His jersey was stripped off his back and people were wearing pieces of it on their lapels for weeks afterwards. Jack was whisked off from the train station in Dublin the next day by a girl in a sports car whom he had never met, but who was sporting a piece of his jersey on her blouse. He stayed with her for a week and lost his job when he went back to London.

OUR WILLIE IS BIGGER THAN YOUR CONDOM

In sporting terms he is one of a kind. Willie Anderson is famous in the rugby world for playing the bagpipes. Whatever that indefinable quality called charisma is, this guy has it in buckets.

As a player Anderson had many highs and lows, the highs being the 1985 Triple Crown and the night he captained a scrap Irish side to a famous victory over France at Auch in 1988 – Ireland's only victory over France on French territory in over twenty years.

His appearances against France were memorable for his epic struggles with the French lock, Jean Condom. Hence the banner that appeared in the crowd in Lansdowne Road at the Ireland–France match in 1985: 'Our Willie is bigger than your Condom.'

THE FUTURE KING AND I

After captaining Ireland to a defeat against England, Willie Anderson was talking to Will Carling at the dinner in the Hilton. It was a very serious atmosphere, so he asked Carling to go downstairs with him for a 'wee drink'. Willie asked him what he wanted and Carling said a gin and tonic, so he ordered two. He nearly dropped dead when the barman charged him ten pounds. When he asked him could he charge it to his room the barman said no. Then Willie pulled out two Northern Ireland five pound notes. The barman immediately said he couldn't take these. He said to Carling he would have to pay for the drinks.

Although Ireland lost the match, at least Willie had the satisfaction of making the English captain buy him a drink, which was said to be a more difficult task than beating England.

In the 1990s there was much media speculation about a doomed romance between Princess Diana and England's rugby captain Will Carling. Carling strongly denied the rumours. After news of the alleged affair was leaked to the press, Prince Charles had to present the International Championship trophy to Carling in a match in which the captain failed to get a try. The prince said, 'I'm sorry you didn't score.'

Carling replied: 'At last. Somebody believes me.'

Before Austin Healey took the title, Carling was the England player with an exceptional capacity to rub people up the wrong way. Carling went up to Leicester to play for Harlequins in a league match in a fixture that was being filmed by *Rugby Special*. After the match, Carling was set upon by a Leicester fan who punched him on the chin. It was widely reported afterwards that it was the first time the fan had hit the sh*t.

Carling has a more sociable side. On the Lions tour in 1993 Carling was rechristened 'O'Carling' when he started drinking Guinness.

THE WILL TO WIN

Anderson enjoys the stories about Carling's former marriage to the TV presenter, Julia. After she woke up one morning, Julia said to her husband, 'I just dreamed that you gave me a pearl necklace for our anniversary. What do you think that means?'

'You'll know tonight,' Carling said. That evening he came home with a small package and gave it to his wife. Delighted she opened it – to find a book entitled *The Meaning of Dreams*.

One of Anderson's favourite stories about the former English captain goes back to early in his marriage to Julia when after being away a long time on tour he thought it would be good to bring her a little gift. 'How about some perfume?' he asked the girl in the cosmetics department. She showed him a bottle costing £100, 'That's too much,' he said. The girl then said, 'We do have this smaller bottle for £50.' 'That's still too much,' he said. The girl brought out a tiny £20 bottle, but even that was too costly for him. 'What I mean is,' he said, 'I'd like to see something really cheap.'

The assistant handed him a mirror.

IT'S THE WAY HE TELLS THEM

In the late 1980s Willie Anderson was chosen as captain of Ireland. The downside was that he had to make the speeches at the dinners after matches. A lot of drink is consumed on those occasions and not everyone wants to listen to a speech. One of his earliest dinners as captain was after a Scottish game. During his address he looked down and he could see Kenny Milne with his hand over his mouth trying to hold back the vomit. He could only hope it was from drink and not from listening to his speech.

Willie seemed to have an effect on Scottish players. At another Scottish dinner he was sitting beside Craig Chalmers all night. At the end Chalmers had to be carried away on one of the tables.

Willie cannot be held responsible for all the accidents at Scottish dinners. At a post-match dinner in Cardiff in 1986, the table that the Scottish tight head prop Iain 'The Bear' Milne was leaning on collapsed. Milne's response was to say, 'Waiter, bring me another table.'

As a forward, Milne did not enjoy the expansive game. In 1988 he was asked if he was happy that the pitch was just right for fast, open, running rugby. Milne's reply was, 'The conditions are bloody awful.'

RUBBING THEIR NOSES IN IT

For years the All Blacks have tried to intimidate opponents by performing the haka:

Ka mate!/Ka mate!/Ka Ora/Ka Ora/Tēnei te tangatapūhuruhuru/ Nāna i tiki mai whakawhiti te rā/A Upane!/Ka Upane!/A Upane Kaupane/Whiti te rā!/Hī! (I die, I die / I live, I live / This is the hairy man / Who caused the sun to shine again for me / Up the ladder! Up the ladder / Up to the top / The sun shines! Rise!)

No All Black game would be complete without it. As a norm, the opposition react by not reacting and feigning indifference. One man though was determined to do otherwise.

During the haka, before Ireland played the All Blacks in 1989, Willie Anderson led the Irish team right up to the noses of the New Zealanders in an effort to intimidate them.

Anderson told me about the fear:

'It was a joint effort between myself and our coach Jimmy Davidson.'

After the match Wayne Shelford was asked if he was scared. He said he was absolutely petrified. When asked why, he said: "I was terrified that Willie Anderson was going to kiss me."'

A RIPE, OLD AGE

In 1985, after Ireland famously beat England to win the Triple Crown, Willie Anderson's wife, Heather, met the wife of the future Nobel Prize winner for Literature, Seamus Heaney, which was a big thrill for Heather as she is an English teacher. A few weeks afterwards they were at the dinner to mark the Triple Crown victory. It was the night of one of Barry McGuigan's big fights and Willie went upstairs to see the contest on the television. Heather was there on her own and was trying to make polite conversation. She was chatting to Ciaran Fitzgerald and made a bit of a *faux pas* by telling him that she had met James Joyce's wife after the English match. Fitzie turned around and asked Hugo MacNeill what age would Mrs Joyce be. Hugo answered, 'About 150.'

SPEED SOUGHT

Willie had a great affection for the coach of that team, Mick Doyle:

'Doyler had a wicked sense of humour. He was taking us for a Sunday morning training session. His prop forward Jim McCoy was not moving as swiftly as Doyler would have liked. Big Jim was an RUC officer and brought up in the Protestant tradition. Doyler shouted at him, "Hurry up McCoy or you'll be late for Mass."'

MAMMY'S BOY

Anderson loved the joy of rugby:

'Even when things are at their blackest from a rugby point of view there are always moments of comedy on tour. After we lost to Australia in the World Cup in 1987 Donal Lenihan rang home. As a result of the time difference the match was shown live on Irish television at 6 a.m. His mother had seen the match and knew the result already. Instead of offering him sympathy she said, "Anyone stupid enough to play rugby at 6 o'clock in the morning deserves to lose!"'

THE NUMBERS GAME

Like David Campese, Anderson believes in having an upbeat attitude to rugby and life, which is typified in the story of the man at his 103rd birthday party who was asked if he planned to be around for his 104th.

'I certainly do,' he replied. 'Statistics show that very few people die between the ages of 103 and 104.'

THE STAR OF DAVID

David Humphreys has many happy memories of his time playing with Ulster:

'Probably my favourite rugby story goes back to 2003, just before the World Cup. The international players were away with the Irish squad and Johnny Bell was made captain of Ulster for a Celtic League match. Just before the game Johnny gathered all the players around him, brought them into a huddle and said: "Right lads, there's just two things I want from you in this game." He paused dramatically. You could almost cut the tension with a knife as he said: "Honesty, commitment and work rate." The lads almost fell on the floor laughing at his gaffe. Ulster lost badly and Johnny's career as a captain came to an abrupt and undistinguished end.'

ULSTER SAYS YES

In 1999 Ulster won the European Cup final in Lansdowne Road. All of Ireland got behind Ulster, bidding to become the first Irish side to win the competition. A number of prominent Ulster Unionist politicians were at Lansdowne Road for the occasion. One found himself in the proximity of a staunch republican who was very much on the opposite end of the spectrum in terms of attitude to Northern Ireland. The Unionist turned to this staunch Nationalist and said, 'How does it feel to belong to a thirty-two county Ulster?'

LAST ORDERS

Ulster lock Jeremy Davidson was dubbed 'Dangerous' on the Lions tour in 1997 because he seemed to injure player after player. Matt Dawson recalls touring with Davidson. The two of them were joined by Neil Back and went to a bar in a remote part of Pretoria. They stood drinking so long that the barman asked them to lock the door when they left.

LIKE A BRIDGE OVER TROUBLED WATER

One of Mick Galwey's biggest rivals for a place in the Irish second row was Ulster's Paddy Johns. Johns was a dentist by profession. Galwey once joked that Paddy's motto was: 'We can floss that bridge when we come to it.'

PATTY

Colin Patterson's short career with Instonians, Ireland and the Lions ended prematurely because of injury. He still remains one of Ireland's greatest ever scrum halves, even if his stay in the green jersey was all too short.

Patty was a big admirer of Ollie Campbell's dedication. When Ollie came into the Irish squad he and Mike Gibson would stay on the pitch on their own for extra training. Patty claims that since they didn't drink they had nothing else to do!

WELSH WISDOM

Patterson told me about one of his favourite trips. The 1980 Lions tour took place in the era when you paid for your own telephone calls home. The Welsh players had devised three great tricks so they never had to pay for a telephone call. Plan A was to charm the hotel receptionist into giving them the secret code they could use to make calls without having them charged to them. Plan B was to distract the receptionist and for one of them to sneak in behind the desk and steal all their telephone bills. Plan C was to allow a journalist to have an interview in exchange for a phone call.

Best of all for getting freebies though was when they went into the Adidas factory. Each player was allowed to pick a bag of their choice and stuff it with gear. Most players selected the most stylish bags and filled them with gear. All the Welsh guys, without exception, took the biggest bags in the shop and walked out with half of the gear in the factory.

In 1983 when the Scottish players were chosen to tour with the Lions to New Zealand the advice Patty gave them was: 'Be sure and stay close to the Welsh when they visit the Adidas factory.'

Born not to sing

Tony Ward was Colin's first half back partner with Ireland. As an Ulsterman, Patterson was not brought up in the Nationalist tradition so Ward had the job of teaching Colin the national anthem. In the interests of political balance Patterson sang the first half of the Irish anthem and for the second half he sang the anthem of Unionism, *The Sash My Father Wore*. Ward claims that listening to Patterson singing never failed to bring a tear to his eye. Patterson's singing really was that bad.

It started on the Late Late Show

Patty made his impact in the media:

'I later went on *The Late Late Show* with Tony Ward when he was the golden boy of Irish rugby, and landed him in big trouble. Gay Byrne asked us if we had thought about defecting to Rugby League. When Tony rejected the idea out of hand Gay turned to me and said:

'"Tony is looking down on Rugby League, Colin, how about you?"

'"When you are only five foot five inches you can't afford to look down on anything," I replied.

'The personality differences between Tony and I were also very evident on that visit. We were both asked what we would like to drink. I said two Irish coffees please, which was not what they normally provided and would take a bit of trouble on their part. Immediately Tony intervened and said:

'"Oh no. Don't go to any trouble for us."

'"Okay Tony, I'll drink yours as well," I answered, and we both got our Irish coffees.'

Ireland's Next Top Model

Patterson never missed an opportunity to poke fun at his teammate. 'I loved winding Tony up. Of course he gave me the ideal opportunity after the publication of his Page Three-style pose in his swimming trunks before the Scottish game in 1979. I pinned up the photo on the wall and kept gushing to him about his fantastic bum and how no woman could possibly resist him.'

Knick-knack paddywhack

Patterson observed the sensational decision to drop Ward for Campbell from close quarters on Ireland's tour to Australia in 1979:

'People kept asking me why he was dropped. There were all kinds of speculation, including the ridiculous notion that Wardy was caught in bed with one of the selectors' wives. Tony is not like that. I think that the essential difference between Tony and Ollie was that Tony, like myself, was an inside runner whereas Ollie was an outside runner. As both were superb kickers I feel it made for a better balance to have an inside and outside runner playing at half backs.

'The Tuesday before the first Test we were playing Queensland, but Tony and I had been told we would not be playing. I saw the other scrum half Johnny Moloney on the morning of the game and he was fit and well so I knew I could relax. I ordered a big fillet steak and egg for my meal. Shortly afterwards Noel Murphy came to me and told me I was playing. I told him to get lost and not to be kidding me because I had seen Moloney that morning and he was fine. Then Noisy said: "Johnny's on the wing." My steak started wobbling in my stomach, but I would have to play. Myself and Ollie played well in what was effectively a Test match and we won. After the match there were a lot of barbecues. We were watching them from out or window and started singing *Waltzing Matilda.* The Aussies began throwing beer cans at us but we had the last laugh because many of the cans were half full so we grabbed the cans, drank the beer and threw the cans back at them.

'After the storm about Wardy being dropped off the team the Australian press rubbished our chances of winning the first Test. One headline read: *Ireland to be Paddywhacked into Rugby Oblivion.* We beat them 27–12. If ever a victory was sweet, this was it. The place went berserk. I have a picture at home, taken in the dressing room which shows Ollie and I together, grinning from ear to ear. It was such a turn-up for the books.'

WHERE DID IT ALL GO WRONG?

After Ireland's success in Australia they were confidently expected to take the Triple Crown the next season. With his tongue firmly in his cheek, Patty offers an unusual explanation for Ireland's failure to do so.

'We should have won the Triple Crown in 1980. I blame Ollie Campbell. Although we defeated Scotland and Wales we lost to England. At one stage Jim Glennon was bursting through and we had the overlap with Ollie on one side and me on the other. I was certain I was going to score a try, but the ball went to Campbell and not me and he fluffed it. It's time he was de-canonised.'

THE RIGHT STUFF

With his small stature Patterson was an obvious target for intimidation on the rugby pitch:

'I prided myself on my ability to take punishment. The tougher it got the better I liked it. Whenever I got crushed by somebody I got up immediately and said to him "Good tackle soldier," which really annoyed them. At internationals there were a number of efforts to verbally intimidate me. I never let that sort of bullsh*t get to me. The best example of this was when we played Wales in 1980. Where Stuart Lane wasn't going to stuff the ball up my anatomy, I can't say. I eventually turned around and said to him: "Stuart you don't mean that." It was my last home game for Ireland, so the BBC gave me the video of the match. When I watched it I saw again Stuart bursting into laughter and saying: "You're a cheeky wee bo***cks." The more a player tried to intimidate me the more I wound him up by waving at him in the line-out and so on. Apart from the fact that it helped me to win the psychological war, it's the only fun us small fellas get.'

GONE TOO SOON

In 1980 tragedy swooped like a hawk flying down from the sky when Patterson's career was prematurely ended on the Lions tour to South Africa. It was one of those moments when sadness and joy share the narrow path of life. Patty was at the height of his powers when all was taken from him in an accidental clash.

'It all began with an innocuous incident. I was screaming in agony; the pain was so intense. My situation was not helped by the fact that the referee tried to play amateur doctor with me and started poking around with my leg. I was stretchered off, but they are so fanatical about their rugby out there that two fans rushed on. One took my discarded boot and the other my sock and he asked me if I would give him my shorts.'

For all of that, Patterson has many happy memories of his time with the Lions.

'It was a real education touring with the Welsh. One night they did a classic wind-up on the English player Mike Slemen, who was the leading try scorer on the tour. All of them gathered into the one room and rang Mike up pretending to be from the BBC World Service, with a suitably posh accent. They fed him a lot of compliments and he started blowing his own trumpet and claimed that he probably was one of the best players on the tour. Eventually the Welsh lads could take no more and shouted: "Slemen you're a useless f**ker." The English man was mortified that he had been caught out so badly.'

WATCH IT

Patty had a memorable moment after the third Test in Port Elizabeth. The Lions had gone into the game two down, and so it was the decider. In shocking weather the Lions lost 12–10, and thereby the series. The Lions were very disappointed – it was a game that had been won everywhere but on the scoreboard. Still, there was no sulking. In the best tradition, the Lions decided to drown their sorrows, and so a monumental p***-up was held. A few equally drunk South African fans had found their way into the hotel's off limits area, and a bit of a skirmish developed. At one stage the Lions manager Jack Matthews chucked a couple of the intruders down the stairs. He picked up a watch off the ground and flung it down after the guys, with a cry of: "And take your blasted watch with you." Then he saw his bare wrist: in the excitement he had flung his own watch down the stairs.

GENTLEMAN JIM

The late Jimmy Davidson was a much loved Ulster coach. As a player, the high point of Jimmy's career was on Ireland's tour to New Zealand in 1976 when he was called in for the Irish side as a replacement. He was so happy to be selected that he jumped for joy when he got on the team bus for the first time. He jumped so high that he smashed his head against the roof and needed six stitches. For his first game on the tour the Irish were worried about things getting out of hand on the pitch. At one stage there was a melee in the ruck and Pa Whelan mistakenly stamped Davidson on the head. Initially the Irish lads thought one of the New Zealand guys had done it and there was bedlam for two minutes. When order was restored the first thing the Irish players heard was Davidson shouting at his own teammate, who had been responsible for the injury: 'You f**king idiot Whelan.' After the game Davidson needed multiple stitches.

Full moon

John Robbie was the youngest player in the Irish party, and he looked it. On one boat trip during the tour, some New Zealander glanced at him and remarked, in all seriousness, that it was nice of the New Zealand rugby union to allow the Irish manager to bring his son along on tour.

On the last game of the tour Ireland played Fiji. The Fijians were lovely people, but there was a bit of an incident after the game between an Irish player and one of theirs. When asked about the resolution of the incident the Irish player, who shall remain nameless, said frankly: 'I gave him a black eye.'

The Irish team travelled throughout the island in an old bus with no windows. John Robbie got a bit drunk after the game. He had told the team about the craze at the time of 'lobbing moons' – pulling one's trousers down, bending over and displaying the bare backside to all and sundry. The trick was to choose the time and the place with the most care to get the greatest effect. The Fijian bus without windows was too much of a temptation, and so Robbie lobbed a moon. The locals were totally amazed. Suddenly the Irish players heard an anguished scream. It was Robbie shouting: 'My God, I've lobbed my wallet.' It had fallen out the window, and Christmas had come early for some lucky local.

Musings

Jimmy Davidson was also an amateur philosopher. Hence his comment:

'Rugby is the only game where a man sticks his head up another man's bum and the referee allows it.'

He also loved the characters of the game. A case in point is Sam Hutton of Malone, not least because of his famous chat-up line: 'Excuse me darling, haven't you met me somewhere before?'

EVERYBODY LOVES GOOD NEIGHBOURS

Davidson enjoyed the great rivalry that existed between Ulster and Leinster. One of his favourite stories was about the suspicious Belfast rugby fan who hired a private eye to check on the movements of his wife. In addition to a written report, the husband wanted a video of his wife's activities. A week later, the detective returned with a film. They sat down together and proceeded to watch it. Although the quality was less than professional, the man saw his wife meeting another man. He saw the two of them strolling arm in arm and laughing in the park. He saw them enjoying themselves at an outdoor café. He saw them dancing in a dimly-lit nightclub before embarking on more erotic adventures in a hotel afterwards. He saw them take part in a dozen activities with utter glee. 'I just can't believe this,' said the distraught husband.

'What's not to believe?' the detective said. 'It's right up there on the screen.'

The husband replied, 'I simply can't believe my wife would disgrace me by wearing a Leinster jersey in public.'

DIPLOMATIC SKILLS

Another Davidson favourite concerned Michael Lynagh, George Gregan and David Campese, who were watching an Australian match from the roof of the stadium. Lynagh fell off and was killed instantly. As the ambulance took the body away, Gregan said, 'Someone should go and tell his wife.'

Campese said, 'Okay, I'm pretty good at that sensitive stuff, I'll do it.'

Two hours later he came back carrying a case of Fosters.

Gregan asked, 'Where did you get that, Campo?'

'Michael's wife gave it to me.'

Gregan replied, 'That's unbelievable, you told that lady her husband was dead and she gave you the beer?'

'Well, not exactly,' Campo said. 'When she answered the door, I said to her, "You must be Michael's widow."

'She said, "No, I'm not a widow."

'And I replied, "I'll bet you a case of Fosters you are."'

THE LION KING

The most successful British Lions team of all time was that which toured South Africa in 1974 and made Willie John McBride, their captain, an icon of the game. Their overall record in their twenty-two matches read: won twenty-one, drew one, lost none, points for 729, points against 207. After their 12–3 victory in the first Test, skipper McBride warned his fellow forwards to expect a bruising encounter: 'You've not seen anything yet. They will throw everything at you, even the kitchen sink.'

One night on the tour a group of players were partying in their hotel in the middle of the night. An undiplomatic war broke out. The tiny hotel manager tried to keep the peace. Two scantily-clad players were parading around the corridors and he roared at them to get back into their rooms. Not liking his attitude, they told him with all due lack of politeness what to do with himself. The manager's threat to ring the police met with no reaction. Then along came Willie John McBride. The manager thought his problems were solved at the sight of the Lions captain arriving. When McBride seemed to be ignoring the matter the manager repeated his threat to call the police. Willie John called him forward with a tilt of his head. The manager breathed a sigh of relief. His threat had worked. He was in for a big disappointment as McBride bent down to him and whispered, 'How many will there be?'

Willie John went back to the party. Some time later a group of riot police arrived with their dogs. Again Willie John intervened decisively. He went down to the coffee machine and bought some milk and gave it to the dogs and then invited the police to join the party. They did, and had the night of their lives.

DEAD OR ALIVE?

When the Lions won the series in 1974 a magnificent party was staged in the hotel. The festive spirit got a little out of hand, and every fire extinguisher and water hose in the hotel was set off. The problem was that nobody thought to turn them off. The result was that the next morning the hotel could have done with the services of Noah's Ark. The touring manager was summoned the next morning to explain the actions of his team. He had gone to bed early and had no idea what was happening until he discovered himself thigh deep in water. He half walked, half swam up to Willie John's room and prepared to knock on the door only to discover that the door had been a casualty of the flood. To his astonishment, McBride was calmly sitting on his bed as it bobbed around on the water, putting contentedly on his pipe. The manager lost control and launched into a viscous tirade. Finally, Willie John replied, 'Alan, can I ask you one question?'

'What?'

'Is there anybody dead?'

BLACK COFFEE

One day on tour in South Africa, McBride and Andy Irvine went into a diner that looked as though it had seen better days. As they slid in to a booth, Irvine wiped some crumbs from the seat. Then he took a napkin and wiped some mustard from the table. The waitress, in a dirty uniform, came over and asked if they wanted some menus.

'No thanks,' said Andy, 'I'll just have a cup of black coffee.'

'I'll have a black coffee, too,' Willie John said. 'And please make sure the cup is clean.'

The waitress shot him a nasty look. She turned and marched off into the kitchen. Two minutes later, she was back.

'Two cups of black coffee,' she announced. 'Which of you wanted the clean cup?'

MEDICALLY BEWILDERING

Irish hooker Ken Kennedy had a dramatic introduction to the Lions tour to South Africa in 1974. Although travelling as a player, it was Kennedy's medical skills which were first called for when Bobby Windsor was taken ill with food poisoning. He was so ill that he was taken to the back of the plane and told to suck ice cubes to help him cool down. As team doctor Kennedy came to take his temperature, without knowing about the ice cubes. When he looked at the thermometer he shouted out: 'Jaysus, Bobby you died twenty-four hours ago.'

'EAR 'EAR

Inevitably when talking of front rows, the famous Pontypool front row of Charlie Faulkner, Bobby Windsor and Graham Price, celebrated in song and folklore by Max Boyce, looms large for Kennedy. The camaraderie between front row players is amazing, especially between the Pontypool gang. It is a strange fact of rugby life that people in the same positions on the field tend to pal around together. It was said that Windsor's tactic with novice opponents was to bite them on the ear early in the match and say: 'Behave yourself, son, and nothing will happen to this ear of yours.'

Windsor was one of the game's great raconteurs. One of his favourite stories was about a Welsh Valleys rugby club on tour in America. On coming back from a night on the town, two of the players could not find their rooms. They decided to check for their teammates by looking through the keyholes. At one stage they came on an astonishing sight. There in her birthday suit was a Marilyn Monroe lookalike. Close by was a man who was chanting out with great conviction: 'Your face is so beautiful that I will have it painted in gold. Your breasts are so magnificent that I will have them painted in silver. Your legs are so shapely that I will have them painted in platinum.' Outside the two Welsh men were getting very aroused and began jostling each other for the right of the keyhole. The man inside hearing the racked shouted out: 'Who the hell is out there?' The two Welsh men replied: 'We're two painters from Pontypool.'

So macho

Mick Doyle was one of the many players to pay homage to Ken Kennedy:

'The great thing about my rugby career was that it gave me the opportunity to meet so many great characters, like Ken Kennedy. He has a great irreverence. I would describe him as a macho David Norris. I have great respect for him as a person and he was an incredible player.'

Safety first

Ken Kennedy was a top doctor as well as a top hooker. According to folklore when he was asked during a gynaecology lecture: 'When is the safe period?'

He replied: 'Half-time when Ireland play Wales in Cardiff Arms Park.'

Delivery service

Kennedy's Ulster teammate Stewart McKinney tells a great story about Johnny Murphy. Murphy was collecting the flanker for a London Irish match in London. As usual, he was late and McKinney was hassling him for being tardy and telling him that he needed the time for a really good warm-up. Before they got to the ground Murphy pulled up the car sharply and McKinney assumed there was an emergency when his driver asked him to jump out. He duly did so, only to find his bag thrown out after him. Murphy shouted: 'Run the last f**king mile to the ground and you'll be nicely warmed up.'

LET US PRAY

It wouldn't be accurate to say the Irish team were an ecumenical bunch, but there were times religion brought them together. Ireland became the first team from the Northern Hemisphere to beat Australia on home soil in 1967. After winning their Saturday match, the boys in green had a great celebration and all went to Mass on the Sunday evening. One of the lads feel asleep and during the most solemn point of the Mass he suddenly shouted out from his slumber: 'Hallelujah.'

On the tour to New Zealand in 1976 the team doctor, Dr Bob O'Connell, organised Mass at Palmerston North for the Irish team on a holy day of obligation for Catholics. They could not get Mass anywhere so it was decided to invite a priest along. The Catholics knew to bring change for the collection but the others didn't, with the result that the priest got a silent, generous collection from the Protestants. He was thrilled, and wrote to all the Irish papers telling them what a wonderful bunch the Irish squad were and such fabulous ambassadors for their country.

CHAPTER SIX

The Best of the West

Connacht has produced some exceptional players down through the years, like Ray McLoughlin, Ciaran Fitzgerald, John O'Driscoll, Mick Molloy, Eric Elwood, and the tradition continues with the recent rise to prominence of Robbie Henshaw. They have shown the rugby world that when all beside a vigil keep, the West's awake! Apart from their unceasing curiosity as 'words of wisdom', rugby stories enable us to peer through the glass darkly, as it were, and glimpse the attitudes and philosophies of its practitioners. Rugby's verbal legacy invariably reflects a high sophistication, mature wisdom and a cultivated social sense, and serves as an invaluable sociological barometer and cultural index. If this sounds very serious it is because it is a blatant effort to give some spurious status to the following light-hearted romp through decades of rugby tomfoolery. In this chapter rugby's high and mighty do not escape the barb, but there is much here to remind us why the west is best.

NOT SIMPLE SIMON

Neither Connacht nor Ireland has ever produced a more thrilling winger than Simon Geoghegan. His misfortune was to be on an Irish team that was in something of a slump, although it defies belief that he was not chosen as an automatic selection for the Lions tour in 1993.

Simon was happy though to see his friend Nick Popplewell selected. At one point he was rucking beside Brian Moore. Poppy got a blow to the head and said to Moore: 'I can see two balls and cannot continue.'

Moore replied: 'Get back on the pitch and kick both.'

It would not be Popplewell's last encounter with Moore, who was notorious for trying to outpsych opponents before key internationals. Indeed some of his colleagues on the English team remarked that when he played against France in Paris he was more focused on putting his opponent off than playing his own game. There was one famous occasion when he was hoist with his own petard in Ireland's 13–12 win over England in Twickenham in 1994. The Irish players decided to start a fight with the English team early in the match to throw their opponents off their stride. In the dressing room beforehand the question arose as to who should start the fight. Poppy's eyes turned to Peter Clohessy. When the match started the Claw was looking around for a suitable person to fight with. He first considered Jason Leonard, but he thought Leonard might be a bit of a handful to deal with, so his eyes fell on Brian Moore when there was scrum in front of the English posts. Moore, like Peter Beardsley, is not the most handsome man in the world. One of his teammates said of him, in an alcohol-induced moment, that his front teeth are in the back of his mouth and the back teeth are in the front, and that he was born so ugly that his mother thought his face was on fire and she decided to put it out – with a shovel!

The Claw said to him, 'Listen pal, what are you going to do for a face when Sadam wants his arseh*le back?' Moore immediately started a bust-up, and because he struck the first blow Ireland got a penalty and three easy points.

THE BEST OF THE WEST

ALL RISE

The 1993 Lions tour left Popplewell with many happy moments. It is important to have light moments on a tour whether it is with club, country or the Lions. Nicknames are one way of keeping up the levity. Another effort to break the monotony on a rugby tour is 'a court session', where players are judged by their peers and given an appropriate punishment for their transgressions. They generally involve taking in more than a modicum of alcohol.

On the 1993 tour, Judge Paul Rendall sentenced Scott Hastings to listen to two hours of Richard Clayderman tapes on his personal stereo after being found guilty of having his hair cut in a style that was 'an affront to what little hair Graham Dawe had left'. At one stage on that tour Nick Popplewell was the judge, Stuart Barnes was the defending barrister and Brian Moore was the prosecutor. Things got unexpectedly serious one night before the first Test when Moore suddenly started talking about tactics. He said: 'I've got an idea to improve our chances on this tour.'

Barnes immediately said: 'Great. When are you leaving?'

LOVE AND MARRIAGE

Simon Geoghegan got to experience Barnes' unique sense of humour when he played for Bath. In 1990 Bath beat old rivals Gloucester 6–3 in a closely fought match to reach the Pilkington Cup final. After the game the Bath players and their significant others retreated to the Rec for a celebration. Barnes was chatting with one of the supporters and offered to buy him a drink. 'What would you like?'

The fan thought he was in heaven to have a drink bought by the Bath captain and replied, 'I'd like something tall, cold and full of gin.'

'Then come and meet my wife,' answered Barnes.

Bath, at the time, was the team with all the talents. At the time they even tried to sign David Campese, but even their resources could not stretch to Campo's salary demands. The joke was that Campese was either going to play in France for the Cannes Openers or in China for the Peking Toms.

Geoghegan enjoyed the folklore about the giants of Bath rugby at the time. After their summer break Simon was talking to the English fly-half Simon Barnes about his trip to Switzerland. In particular he asked Barnes if he had enjoyed the beautiful scenery.

'Not really,' Barnes replied, 'I couldn't see much because of all the mountains in the way.'

Write here

Another teammate on that team was Jeremy Guscott. Guscott was walking down the centre of Bath one day when an old man stopped him and held out a paper and pen. Jeremy gave him his best smile and assumed it was for an autograph. His ego took a bit of a blow when the old man said: 'Can you address this post card for me? My arthritis is acting up and I can't even hold a pen.'

'Certainly, sir,' said Guscott. He wrote out the address and also agreed to write a short message and sign the card for the man. Finally he asked, 'Now, is there anything else I can do for you?'

The old man said, 'Yes, at the end could you just add, "PS: Please excuse the sloppy handwriting"?'

Camera angle

Mick Doyle was not a man to lavish praise on the Irish team with wanton abandon, so when he described an Irish victory as an 'eighty minute orgasm' one had to sit up and take notice. The performance which prompted this vintage 'Doylerism' was Ireland's 17–3 victory over England in 1993.

Still basking in the glory of their win over the All Blacks, the English expected to extract retribution in 1994 in Twickenham but a splendid try from Simon Geoghegan helped Ireland to secure another shock win – this time on a score of 13–12. During these years the Underwood brothers played on the wings for England. Whenever either scored a try, the Director of the BBC coverage of the English game always cut to the stands where invariably their mother was dancing a jig with elation. After scything past Tony Underwood to score that try Simon is said to have turned to Underwood and remarked: 'I hope your mother saw that!'

Another famous quip is former Irish international Trevor Brennan's remark to referee Alan Lewis: 'It's not a sin bin you need it's a skip.'

Neil down

Tragically, injury brought Geoghegan's career to a premature end and Irish and world rugby were deprived of one of its most thrilling wingers. Geoghegan's performance was not always enhanced by his Irish teammates. He was rooming with Neil Francis the night before the Fiji game in November 1995, Murray Kidd's first outing as team coach. Francis got thirsty during the night and downed a glass of water in the bathroom. The next morning when Geoghegan went to retrieve his contact lenses he discovered that Francis had unwittingly drunk them and the glass of water.

Number two to the number two

As Warren Gatland proved with Wales' victory over Ireland in 2015, you write him off at your peril. He began his coaching career with Connacht. As a player he was in the right place at the wrong time. He established himself as the number two All Blacks hooker. The only problem was that Sean Fitzpatrick was the number one!

As a coach Gatland had more opportunities to shine. Before taking Wasps to the summit of British rugby, Gatland was in charge of Ireland. Peter 'the Claw' Clohessy sometimes had problems deciphering Gatland's Kiwi accent. On tour to Australia the Claw was having trouble sleeping and Gatland suggested he take a sleeping pill before the second Test. The morning of the game Gatland asked the Claw how he had slept. Claw replied, 'Great.'

'Did you take a pill?' asked Gatland.

The Claw looked very sheepish as he replied, 'Yeah, yeah I did.'

'Did you get one off the doc?'

'What?'

'Did you get a sleeping pill off the Doc?'

'Aw, f**k, is that what you meant? I thought you'd asked me if I'd had a pull, not a pill.'

NUMERICALLY CHALLENGED

Gatland also tells the story of how one day Trevor Brennan came to him in training and said he was feeling a bit tired and wondered if he had any suggestions. Gatland replied, 'Take four or five bananas and that should help.' The next morning Trevor went up to apologise profusely, 'Gats, I'm sorry I could only manage twenty-nine bananas.'

Gatland shook his head as he said, 'Trevor I said four or five bananas, not forty-five!'

FAST EDDIE

Nicknames are an integral part of rugby culture. Rob Andrew's nickname was 'Squeaky' because he never did anything wrong. Given that his waistline was less than trim, Stuart Barnes was known as 'the Barrel'. Some names are not very flattering. Jason Robinson, one of the stars of England's 2003 triumph was often called 'Bible basher' because he is a born-again Christian. Mind you, others call him 'McDonald's' because of his love of junk food. Austin Healey was known as 'Melon Head' when he was young because of his big forehead. Scott Gibbs, a key player for Wales and the Lions, was nicknamed 'Car Crash' because he did not tackle people, he obliterated them. The former English hooker Steve Thompson was called 'Shrek' because of his ... distinctive features.

Terry Kennedy's nickname was 'the Rat'. Everybody in rugby knows this but very few know its origins. On St Mary's tour to Russia in 1977, J. B. Sweeney, who was a great stalwart of the club, christened Kennedy 'Ratskinski' and it was then abbreviated. Hence 'the Rat'. Shane Byrne was known as 'mullet' because of his distinctive hairstyle.

Eddie O'Sullivan has three nicknames. He trained as a PE teacher in Limerick and played a lot of indoor soccer there. As he was a very incisive player he got the nickname 'the dagger'. People have used that against him since he 'replaced' Warren Gatland as Ireland coach. When he went to Garryowen as a player he did a lot of weight training which was very unusual in the 1970s though now its par for the course in rugby. His teammates did not think he was doing weights for rugby reasons so they called him, 'the Beach boy'. He played on the wing with Garryowen and he was pretty quick, so some people called him, 'Fast Eddie'.

I DON'T HAVE A WOOD-EN HEART

Welsh great J. P. R. Williams claims that 'whinging is the constant companion of losers'. It is an occupational hazard for all managers at the highest level given the stresses they are subject to. At the press conference after he was appointed QPR manager, Neil Warnock was asked: 'You're the sixth manager in a year, how are you going to go about the job?'

Warnock: 'I think I'll be renting a house not buying one.'

Eddie O'Sullivan may have been a little surprised when Keith Wood said after his retirement: 'I think I'll take a step away from the game for a while. I don't have the temperament to be a coach. I've known that for a while. Eddie may be a cranky man, but he is not quite as cranky as I am.'

NO ICE, ICE BABY

Eddie O'Sullivan believed in attention to detail. His philosophy was akin to that of Abraham Lincoln – if he had a hundred hours to cut down a tree he would spend ninety-nine hours sharpening the axe. In 2002, O'Sullivan led the Ireland rugby team to Siberia to play a match in an area renowned for its freezing temperatures. As the players are a very pampered lot they can normally get everything they need. Incredibly, on this trip they found there was one thing they couldn't get – ice cubes!

GREAT EXPECTATIONS

In the run-up to the 2007 World Cup some fans were having difficulty accepting the verdict of the experts who predicted that Ireland would do well in the World Cup. To redress the balance they told a story about Eddie O'Sullivan.

In the middle of the night Eddie was woken up by a call from his local garda station in Galway. 'I'm afraid the trophy room has been broken into, sir.' Horrified, O'Sullivan asked, 'Did the thieves get the cups?' 'No, sir,' replied the garda, 'they didn't go into the kitchen.'

One day Eddie was walking along a beach when he came across a bottle. When he unscrewed the top a genie appeared and said, 'I'm so grateful to get out of that bottle that I will grant you one wish.' O'Sullivan thought for a moment and said, 'I have always dreamed that there could be a motorway from outside my front door all the way to Lansdowne Road.' The genie thought for a moment and then said, 'I'm sorry, I can't do that. Just think of all the bureaucracy and red tape involved and all the local authorities who would have to be involved in putting that together. I'm sorry, but could you ask for an easier wish?'

Eddie said, 'Well there is one other thing. I'd like to coach Ireland to win the World Cup.'

The genie thought about it for a few minutes and then said, 'So do you want two lanes or four on that motorway?'

Brothers in arms

One of the giants of Irish rugby is Ray McLoughlin. Ray's brother Feidlim also played for Ireland. Feidlim modestly said, 'We have forty-one caps between us.' What he neglected to point out was that he had only one and Ray held the remaining forty!

A Ray of hope

Ireland were playing Wales in Lansdowne Road in 1974 when Ray McLoughlin and Willie John McBride combined to leave one of the Welsh forwards a little worse for wear. Gareth Edwards was furious and turned to the miscreants and said: 'I know it was one of you two f**kers who did that and you're going to pay for it before the game is finished.' Willie John just peered down at him and softly asked: 'Gareth, are you speaking to us?'

Within seconds Edwards collapsed in a fit of laughter.

Ray McLoughlin loved the many characters he played with on the Irish team such as Bill 'Wigs' Mulcahy who toured with the Lions in 1959. When they played Auckland, Albie Pryor was lining out for the home side and stamped on David Marques' head. To Mulcahy's astonishment, Marques stood up and shook Pryor's hand. After the match Wigs asked Marques why he did that and was even more surprised to hear: 'You wouldn't understand, you're Irish. I shook his hand and called him a cad to make him feel small.'

Wigs was not impressed by either his sportsmanship or his

interest in educating the colonies and witheringly dismissed him: 'With an attitude like that, no wonder you lost the British Empire.'

MIGHTY MOUSE

Ray McLoughlin gloried in his front row jousts with the Scottish prop Ian 'Mighty Mouse' McLauchlan. On the 1974 Lions tour to South Africa the visitors were playing Transvaal. Their tighthead prop was Johan Hendrik Potgieter Strauss, a beast of a man and one of the toughest scrummagers in South Africa. Bobby Windsor wanted to psych him out before the game so he went up to him and asked: 'Are you Johan Strauss?'

'Yes,' the Springbok replied.

Windsor sneered at him dismissively: 'Well, the Mouse will tune your piano for you this afternoon.'

A HOLY SHOW

Rugby tours have a number of striking similarities with a religious pilgrimage, such as uniformity in dress codes, the chanting of familiar songs and a feeling of community and fellowship throughout. The analogy does not hold true for the Wasps tour to Malaysia in 1992 when some of the tourists bared their posteriors for the world to see. Not surprisingly in a Muslim country, this cheeky behaviour caused outrage and the offenders were severely fined and deported.

Rugby tours have a unique capacity to produce tales of the unexpected. Legendary Connacht second row forward Mick Molloy saw some strange sights after he became Irish team doctor. In the World Cup in 1987, co-hosted by Australia and New Zealand, the Irish team was coached by Mick Doyle. Doyler decided he was going to get into shape on the trip because he was two stone overweight. He started to train with the backs and when the lads saw this they stepped up a gear. At the end of the session

Doyler was in bits. Later that night Donal Lenihan heard that he had been taken to hospital. As captain, Donal hopped in a taxi and went to the hospital to see him that evening. He was in the front seat and Syd Millar and Mick Molloy were in the back. At one stage in the conversation, Syd said Mick's wife, Lynne, had been on the phone and was very concerned about him and wanted to come down under to see him. Then he said his girlfriend, Mandy, was very worried about him and she too wanted to travel to see him. The Maori taxi driver turned to Donal and said with real feeling, 'That stuff about holy Catholic Ireland is a load of crap!'

When Donal got back from the hospital Brian Spillane asked, 'Did he have a girl or a boy?' Some years later, at a dinner, Donal told this story to a charming woman with an English accent whom he had never met before, nor had any idea who she was except that she was very well versed in rugby matters. It turned out to be Doyler's ex-wife, Lynne.

BETTER BAD DAYS

In 1981 Ireland lost all four matches in the Five Nations by a single score after leading in all four at half-time. It was Ireland's best ever whitewash! One of the stars of the team was Dr John O'Driscoll who won twenty-six caps from 1978 to 1984, but he was prematurely cast off the Irish team that was whitewashed in 1984.

It was Ray Gravell who called him 'John O'Desperate' on the Lions tour in 1980. The late Welsh legend explained his affection for O'Driscoll to me:

'Ireland supplied two great wing forwards on that Lions tour in Colm Tucker and John O'Driscoll. Colm was such a committed player that it was a pleasure to play with him. I would die for John O'Driscoll. What a player and what a man. Mind you, John and Maurice Colclough were always trying to get me p***ed. They were always pouring rum, without my knowledge, into my soup.

'I will never forget that we played a match a week before the first Test and they sprung this amazing kicker who could kick the ball eighty yards and was really crucifying us. Bill Beaumont said we must do something about him. The next time he kicked the ball I tackled him ferociously and broke his shoulder. John said to me: "Grav, what the f**k are you doing?"

'I replied: "I caught him a late one, early."'

No leap of faith

John O'Driscoll is the consummate gentleman, but he liked to enjoy himself on tour. He was a very committed, driving player, but a real Jekyll and Hyde character. His party piece was to hang out of windows late at night. This got a bit boring after a number of weeks during Ireland's tour of South Africa in 1981. For the sake of variety he decided he would hang someone else out of the window, so one night he dangled Terry Kennedy by the legs as he held him outside the hotel window – seventeen storeys up. It's the only time his teammates had ever seen Terry quiet. Then Willie Duggan came into the room puffing his cigarette, with a bottle of beer in his hand and with his matted hair that hadn't been combed since the tour started. As Willie was such a senior player and a close friend of John's, people assumed he would talk some sense into him. All he said to John before turning and walking out was: 'O'Driscoll, you don't have the guts to let him go.' He was right too.

CHAPTER SEVEN

Rugby's League of Nations

While Ireland has supplied the rugby world with a dispro-portionate amount of great characters, the world of international rugby has not been found wanting for characters either. This chapter pays homage to their greatest hits.

CONFUSION

The 1995 Rugby World Cup final was the subject of a memorable answer on the popular TV programme *A Question of Sport*. Asked who won the final, Phil 'Tuffers' Tufnell replied:

'I know the answer to that one. I'm sure that was the President Nelson Mandela final in South Africa, at the end of apartheid. Didn't Mandela come on the pitch with the blonde fella, you know their captain … François … François Pienaar. Yeah, that's right. Oh, it was the All Blacks wasn't it? That Lomu guy? He scored four tries, ran over everyone, didn't he?

'It was the All Blacks. Yeah, Jonah Lomu won it that year with the All Blacks. No, wait a minute, didn't the All Blacks get food poisoned? Yes, that's right and South Africa won and Nelson Mandela, wearing Pienaar's number seven jersey, presented him with the trophy. Yeah, that's right. And the jumbo jet buzzed the top of the stadium.'

'So,' asked Sue Barker patiently, 'have you got a final answer for us?'

To hysterical laughter in the studio Tuffers replied: 'I have Sue. Australia. I've just had this sudden flash of inspiration. The Wobblies won it that year.'

KNOCK, KNOCK, KNOCKING ON HEAVEN'S DOOR

The 1995 World Cup was Jonah Lomu's tournament. The nineteen-year-old, who weighed twenty-two stone but could run the one hundred metres in eleven seconds and score tries at will, took the rugby world by storm. Lomu made every rugby pitch he graced a theatre of dreams, dwarfing all who trailed in his wake as he scythed through defences. In full flight his handoff gesture is like a royal dismissal to bewildered opponents reduced to looking like oxen on an ice rink.

Jonah Lomu is definitely not the source of this next story, which is often used to highlight what the All Blacks think about England. The All Blacks were playing the English, and after the half-time whistle blew they found they were ahead 70–0, with Jonah Lomu getting ten tries. The rest of the team decided to head for the pub instead of playing the second half, leaving Lomu to go out for the second half on his own.

'No worries,' big Jonah told them. 'I'll join you later and tell you what happened.'

After the game Jonah headed for the pub where he told his teammates the final score: 107–3.

'What?' screamed the irate captain. 'How did you let them get three points?'

Jonah replied apologetically, 'I was sent off with ten minutes to go.'

THAT SINKING FEELING

The All Black fans can give their own team a hard time on those very rare occasions when they sustain a defeat. In the 1999 World

Cup semi-final against France, they led 24–10 in the second half, with the tournament's top try scorer Jonah Lomu scoring two tries and Andrew Mehrtens in excellent kicking form. Between the forty-sixth and fifty-ninth minutes, in the most prolific scoring bursts of rugby history France scored twenty-six points. The All Blacks lost 31–43, with Jeff Wilson scoring a consolation try in the eightieth minute. Some of the All Blacks fans were able to joke that France were the greatest magicians of all time because they made the All Blacks team disappear for thirteen minutes. A new joke was born:

Q. Why aren't the All Black team allowed to own a dog?

A. Because they can't hold onto a lead.

THE OSBORNES

The All Blacks full back in the 1995 World Cup was Glen 'Os' Osborne. Os was not the conventional All Black. Before playing a Test match against France in 1995, Os wanted to get some sleep on the day of the match. The team doctor carefully instructed him that he should only take half a sleeping tablet. Os was not into half measures and took two tablets. He had to be carried into the changing room before the match. When he was eventually woken up, he promptly walked straight into the big mirror, thinking it was another changing room.

There was a row of bottles of all kind of energy drinks laid out on the table. One bottle was clearly labelled 'massage oil' and all the bottles for drinking were bright red. For reasons nobody could ever understand Os decided to take up the massage oil and drink the full bottle. The French had never faced such a slippery customer. He played the game of his life, catching every high ball in sight and scoring a hat-trick of tries.

One evening, a few of the All Black players invited themselves to dinner in Glen's house. After the meal Os said he was going to have a bath. His guests told him they would do the washing-up.

The problem was they couldn't find the washing-up liquid. After searching the kitchen high and low Jonah Lomu was delegated to go into the bathroom to ask Os where it was. When Lomu walked in there were bubbles all over the room. When Jonah asked where the washing-up liquid was: 'Mate, it's here,' and he plucked it out from under all the bubbles.

'What's it doing in the bath?'

'Well I needed some bubbles for my bubble bath.'

WIFE WANTED

In 1987 the All Blacks won the inaugural rugby World Cup final. The country went into a tizzy and tickets for the final were chased with a passion. An advertisement appeared in a magazine in Wellington a few days before the final. 'Young rugby supporter of good appearance and sound health offers hand in marriage to any young lady with two tickets to the World Cup final. Please send photograph of the tickets.'

The All Blacks dominance ensured a bleak time for their old rivals, Australia. This was most obvious on the side of the town bridge in a remote part of Australia where a sign read, 'You are now entering a Nuclear-Free Zone.' A Kiwi fan added a message of his own when he visited the town a few weeks after the final, 'You've now entered a trophy-free zone.'

AN ENGLISHMAN ABROAD

John Gallagher was the only Englishman to win the World Cup before 2003. He played full back for the All Blacks in 1987. He was born in London and didn't go to New Zealand until he was twenty. The Monday after the final he was back at work as a policeman.

At one stage John was invited to attend a major corporate event on the theme of motivation. He sat at the back of the conference hall while the opening speaker gave a most boring speech. Halfway through the speaker noticed his distinguished guest and said, 'If you can't hear me at the back, there is a vacant seat at the front.'

Gallagher replied, 'I can't hear you, but I'm quite happy where I am, thank you.'

Friendly advice

Murray Mexted had many of the traditional strengths of an All Black number eight, but was not your typical dour forward. He was a very colourful personality and talented player. He was very slim with a big knee lift and very hard to knock off the ball. He could play the ball wide or mix it up front. His personality is probably best summed up in a conversation he had with his former teammate, Jamie Salmon. Salmon made history by becoming the first player to be capped for England, having previously being capped for New Zealand. In a quirk of fate, Salmon's England debut was against the All Blacks. Mexted rang Salmon to wish him well and arrange to meet for a drink afterwards. All was sweetness and light until they were exchanging goodbyes when Mexted said: 'Oh, by the way, Jamie, if you come back on the switch during the game, I'll take your f**king head off.'

The body beautiful

Austin Healey, of all rugby players, is very proud of his body, which is why he often paraded around his hotel room naked when he was on tour. When he appeared on *Strictly Come Dancing* he named his biceps 'Con' and 'Crete'.

JUDGE AND JURY

No player on the 1997 Lions tour got more media coverage than Austin 'Oz' Healey. Very little of it was for his contribution on the pitch. His abrasive personality guarantees that he gets under the skin of many people, none more so than some of his teammates. Healey had a major disappointment in 2001 when he failed to make it on the Lions starting team for the Test games. His anger was largely directed against the Lions coach, Graham Henry. Shortly after he returned home Healey bumped into Ian McGeechan, who had coached the Lions to glory on their previous tour. Ian asked, 'Austin, how did the tour go?'

'Oh terrible, terrible. Yer man, Henry, took an instant dislike to me. An instant dislike.'

'Why did he take an instant dislike to you?'

'I suppose he just wanted to save time.'

INJURY TIME

A lengthy injury sustained with Leicester meant that Austin Healey was forced to miss the 2003 World Cup. One of his English teammates was not as sympathetic as might be expected and said: 'Austin's been injured so long we've changed his name to "I can't believe he's not better".'

Healey is nothing if not original. He was brought up to a hearing for stamping on London Irish scrum half Kevin Putt's head. Healey's defence was novel: 'It was the only place I could put my foot.'

DISCRETION IS THE BETTER PART OF VALOUR

In 1999 France toured Argentina for the Mar del Plata Sevens. The French were winning in front of over 30,000 passionate home fans. Prominent international referee Chris White was in charge of proceedings. The stands were separated from the pitch by a moat and a fence, but the teams were still in range of various fruits thrown by the crowd. The French captain was unfortunate enough to go down injured in range of the crowd. White went to check him, but was hit on his calf by a huge orange and had to be treated by a physio. France went on to score a last-minute try to wrap up the match, right in the corner. The kicker walked back for the conversion, right next to the moat, fence and crowd. A barrage of fruit rained down. The terrified French kicker enquired: 'Monsieur Arbite what are you going to do about this?'

White calmly replied: 'I'm going to stand in the middle of the pitch while you take the conversion.'

A MEMORABLE MEMOIR

One of the most famous tours in rugby history was that of the Lions tour to South Africa in 1974. On the pitch, the tour saw some very physical exchanges. One of the props on the tour, Gloucester's Mike Burton was well able to look after himself in these situations. The following year he became the first English international to be sent off in a Test match, following a clash with Australian winger Doug Osborne. In the canon of rugby literature, Burton's autobiography *Never Stay Down* stands out. He devotes a chapter to the best punches he encountered in his career.

RAISE YOUR GLASSES

The night before the first Test in 1993 the Lions were watching the forecast with more keen interest than usual. As the weatherman was giving the details Brian Moore piped up: 'There are an awful lot of isobars about – and I've been in every one of them.'

VIP

Not all rugby tours are pleasurable. Dissatisfaction with facilities is an occupational hazard for rugby tourists. The story is told that on the Lions tour to New Zealand in 1993 the secretary of the touring party, Bob Weighill, asked for an extra pat of butter to accompany his bread roll. He took umbrage when he was told this would not be possible. 'Do you know who I am?' 'No, sir.' The waiter listened impassively as Mr Weighill listed his auspicious catalogue of titles. Then the man softly replied: 'And do you know who I am?'

'No.'

'I'm the man in charge of the butter.'

AGONY UNCLE

On tour to England, David Campese took a taxi back to the team hotel with a few of the other players after a drinking session. The taxi driver was a bit on the larger side and was also 'hygienically-challenged', with a less than enticing aroma emanating from his body. In addition, he recounted a tale of woe about his lack of success with the opposite sex. After the Aussie lads paid their fare the taxi driver said, 'How about a tip?'

Before anyone could even think of reaching into their pockets for a second time Campo interjected, 'Certainly. Start using a deodorant and you might have some chance with the Sheilas.'

LASSIE COME HOME

In the 1990s the great Australian team were on tour. After they got into the airport the whole squad had disembarked and were waiting in the baggage hall, by the carousel. Bags were going around and around, and the players were waiting patiently when they noticed a drugs squad officer with a sniffer dog in tow. He let the dog off the lead and it ran to the carousel and bounded onto the bags, rummaging around. Jason Little was awestruck: 'Isn't that wonderful?'

'Why, Jason?'

'Well, isn't it great, the dog is looking for the blind man's luggage.'

A MISUNDERSTOOD MAN

In 1989 Will Carling was expected to lead England to the Grand Slam, but Wales tripped them up at the last hurdle. The English team had been scheduled to meet England's most famous royal at the time. The equerry of the Princess of Wales came into the English dressing room and said to Carling: 'She'll ask you what your team have said about losing the game and the Grand Slam.'

Carling asked: 'When I'm telling her, do I have to leave out all the cursing and swearing.'

'Certainly.'

'In that case they haven't mentioned it at all.'

Carling has written a number of books, but is unlikely to be writing a book on 'how to win friends and influence people'. Over the years Carling was at the forefront of the debate over the vexed question of whether – and to what extent – rugby should turn professional with all the ferocious protestations and the growing bitterness between administrators and players. This antagonism was graphically revealed in Carling's description of the RFU committee as 'fifty-seven old farts' which caused him to be stripped of the captaincy of the English team.

DAWSON'S PIQUE

Another English international who had problems with officialdom was Matt Dawson. After having a successful tour with the Lions in South Africa in 1997, Matt Dawson went on the Lions tour to Australia in 2001 with high hopes. His great expectations were quickly shattered. His newspaper column spoke of his disenchantment with the team's preparation and criticised the team management. It appeared on the morning of the First Test, and initially it seemed he would be sent home. The threat of banishment hung in the air for a period. Things came to a climax when a crisis meeting was called between players and management. The Lions were captained by Martin Johnson who lived by the creed: minimum amount of words, maximum impact. His brief intervention at the meeting was the decisive one. He simply said that if Dawson was sent home, he would be on the next plane. Issue closed.

Ironically, Dawson got away scot-free from what in the era of Bill Beaumont would be considered a sacking offence for an England rugby international: he shaved his legs, donned a wig and dressed up as woman. What was worse he even did it on national television. The reason for his brief flirtation with cross-dressing was not, as Dan Luger suggested, that he was an apprentice transvestite, but that he was appearing as a mystery guest on the popular BBC series *A Question of Sport*, where top sports people who are up for a laugh routinely embarrass themselves. After his appearance on the programme, his fellow internationals Paul Grayson, Mike Tindall and Ben Cohen claimed that Dawson was the ugliest woman ever to appear on television and threatened not to pay their TV licences in the future in protest.

After England's World Cup victory in 2003, Dawson was one of the English players to cash in by publishing his autobiography, *Nine Lives*. His teammate Mike Catt was reported to be furious because Dawson had 'stolen' the obvious title for his book.

WOODWARD'S WONDERFUL WORLD

England's focus and obsessive will to win the 2003 World Cup can largely be traced back to their coach, Clive Woodward. As a player Woodward won twenty-one English caps, culminating in the 1980

Grand Slam. A stylish outside centre, with wonderful hands, he also toured with the Lions. It was as a coach though that he really excelled.

One of Woodward's favourite phrases is 'massively full on'. This phrase took on a new connotation during the World Cup tournament. Asked how he reacted to being kept awake by chants of 'Boring! Boring!' from Australian fans, he replied: 'I was with my wife in bed at the time – fortunately, I realised what they were actually referring to.'

Woodward was magnanimous in victory after the World Cup final. He did have some reservations about the South African referee Andre Watson's performance in the final, which saw a number of contentious penalties going to Australia. Hence Nick Hancock's comment, 'The World Cup final produced Australia's sports personality of the year – the referee!'

Surprisingly, not everyone in England was eulogising Woodward's team. A rugby league fan wrote to *The Daily Telegraph* and said: 'If rugby union is the game they play in heaven, then God, please send me to hell.'

Go Jonny go

The 2003 World Cup made Jonny Wilkinson the golden boy of English rugby.

Wilkinson's last gasp drop goal against Australia in the World Cup final guaranteed him sporting immortality. Watching the score on a television replay, one could not but be reminded of David Acfield's classic commentary: 'Strangely, in slow motion replay, the ball seemed to hang in the air for even longer.'

Identity crisis

After leading England to the World Cup Martin Johnson triumphantly led his team to Buckingham Palace, where the team had its picture taken with the Queen. Afterwards Johnson said: 'It will be a unique picture with that dog in it.' A spokesman confirmed later that he was referring to a corgi that had run into the shot and not her Majesty.

England's World Cup victory has brought them a whole new profile. This may be a good thing, considering what happened the last time they visited Canada. When they attended a reception one of their hosts enquired: 'It's great to have you soccerball guys here. Which one of you is Beck-Ham?'

SO LONG

At the end of the Six Nations Championship in 2004 another World Cup winner, Jason Leonard, announced his retirement from international rugby. Given his exalted status in world rugby, he might have expected his international colleagues to be full of nostalgia. Austin Healey's reaction to the news was typically edgy: 'I'm sure the lads will be glad to see him gone. There will be more food for everyone else now. He's been their icon of rugby throughout the ages – the stone age, the ice age and the iron age.'

MORE SEX PLEASE. WE'RE BRITISH

In 1977 during the Lions tour to New Zealand, Bobby Windsor was less than impressed by some of the food on offer at an official reception. He made his feelings known to the chef: 'It's not often you get the soup and the wine at the same temperature.'

When the Lions stopped off at a roadside cafe during a long coach drive Windsor complained to the captain Phil Bennett: 'I went into the kitchen here and, do you know, there isn't a single bluebottle in there. They're all married with kids.'

Windsor was even more irate when he tasted the food. He asked the chef: 'What do you do about salmonella?'

The chef replied: 'I fry it in a little batter.'

In the team hotel Bobby one morning was not satisfied about some of the food. At one stage he called over the waiter and said: 'These eggs are awful.'

The waiter casually replied: 'Don't blame me. I only laid the table.'

DEAD RUBBER

Phil 'Benny' Bennett played with the same *joie de vivre* that Brendan Behan had exhibited when he played at Borstal: 'I became a dab hand at this rugby and a bull shoving bast**d at getting the ball back.'

Benny has a host of stories about his Welsh teammates. One day Bobby Windsor approached Bill Clement. Having given sterling service for years to both Wales and the Lions, Bobby decided that the WRU should at least help him with the hire fees for the dinner suit he was obliged to wear at official dinners. So he went to see Clement. Bobby explained how times were hard in the steel industry in Gwent, and, like many others, he had been put on short time. His wife and family were feeling the pinch and every bit of extra cash could help. 'So, if maybe the Union could help me out by hiring the dinner suits then that would be appreciated,' said Windsor.

'I'm sorry,' replied Clement. 'That's against the rules.'

'Well what about my shoes?' said Bobby, getting a bit agitated. 'Surely, you could help me out and allow me to buy a decent pair of shoes to look smart in? These ones are falling apart.' At this juncture, to emphasise the point he took off his shoe and showed Clement how the sole was flapping at the toes. Bill thought about it for a few seconds, and then quietly opened a drawer on his desk marked 'Ticket Money'. He took out a huge bundle of notes and untied them from their tightly wound rubber band. As Bobby was waiting for him to count out the cash, Clement chucked the rubber band over to Windsor and said, 'Here, that should sort out the problem with your shoes.'

JONAH DOESN'T LIVE IN WHALE

In 1997 England played a 26–26 draw with the All Blacks at Twickenham. David Rees scored a try for England and gave a good performance on the wing – even though he faced the apparently impossible task of marking the mighty Jonah Lomu. Before the game Rees had an unusual tactical talk with Clive Woodward. Woodward asked: 'Right Reesy, how are we going to deal with this guy Lomu?'

'Okay, Clive, I'm gonna angle my run so I push him towards the touchline and use it as an extra man, just forcing him out for a line-out.'

'Okay. But what happens if he cuts inside you?'

'Well, I'll angle it so that he's running back towards our cover defence and Kyran Bracken will be there to help smother him and bring him down.'

'Great. But what happens if he runs straight at you?'

'Okay, if he runs straight at me I'll get some crap from the ground and throw it in his face, blinding him.'

'What? But there won't be any crap on the ground.'

'When he's running straight at me, Clive, yes there will.'

SMELLS LIKE?

Hooker Brendan Cannon made his international debut for Australia against the British Lions in 2001. During his career Cannon has faced some memorable opponents in the front row. The strangest one though was an opposition tight head prop in a club game who fell on top of him. He asked Cannon probably the strangest question ever asked in the front row of the scrum: 'That's a nice aftershave you're wearing – what sort is it?'

TOO TOUGH TO SWALLOW

Before the World Cup in 2003, the Aussie press were scornful of the claims that England would win the competition. To illustrate, they told the story of an incident in darkest Africa where there was a river infested with crocodiles. On the other side there was a tribe which various missionaries wanted to convert. However, nobody was willing to take the risk of crossing the river. In Spring 2003, along came a group of missionaries who waded across the river without coming to any harm. Shortly after they revealed their secret. 'We wore T-shirts bearing the words *England – World Cup Champions 2003*. And sure not even a crocodile was willing to swallow that.'

FIGHTING TALK

Australia's inspirational number eight Toutai Kefu was a tough man to tackle. His colleagues sometimes tried too hard to emulate him. One day when he was playing a club match his side was facing defeat. At half-time, the coach roared some fight into them. 'And you Eddie, it's about time you got ferocious.'

'What's his number?' asked Eddie.

Kefu was unwittingly part of some of the great wind-ups of Australian rugby. On his first international tour with the Wallabies to Italy, Kefu was introduced to the president of the Australian Rugby Union, Phil Harry. The other Wallaby players had all told Mr Harry that 'Tongan Bob' – their nickname for Kefu, who was of Tongan extraction – was from a remote Pacific Island village and had only a few words of English. Harry tentatively introduced himself: 'Tou … tai, … me … Phil … Harry … of … Australian … Rugby … Union. Fly … over … on … big … plane … to … watch … you … play. You … played … very … well.'

Harry had completely misinterpreted the look of ever growing bemusement on Kefu's face. In actual fact Kefu had been born and bred in Brisbane, and all the squad collapsed with laughter as Kefu replied uncomfortably: 'Gee, thanks mate.'

A SENSE OF PLACE

The Queensland Reds were on a mini tour in South Africa. They had played the Stormers and were training in Cape Town. Their next opponents were the Blue Bulls in a town called Brakpan. A TV journalist came up and asked the Australian full back Chris Latham for an interview. The request was graciously accepted.

'How do you think your form is at the moment?'

'Yeah, I'm pretty happy with the way things are going. The team is playing well.'

'And a good performance against the Stormers ...'

'Yeah, we're happy the way things are progressing, annoyed to have lost by just a couple of points, but we are concentrating on the next match.'

'So what do you know about Brakpan?'

'Well I reckon he has a pretty good step and a tidy mispass ...'

'Um, um ... actually um ... I'm really sorry Chris, but can we do that last bit again, Brakpan is actually where you are playing.'

'DEAD-EYE DICK'

Naas Botha was one of the most prodigious goal-kickers of all time. Hence the South African's nickname 'Dead-Eye Dick' – a reputation enhanced by his performances against the Lions in 1980. However, he attracted a lot of controversy in South Africa because of his apparent reluctance to pass the ball.

Botha played a club match during a downpour. His team were on top all through the game and Botha was kicking everything. His right winger was going mad for a pass and eventually Botha gave him one, but the winger dropped it and the opposition broke right up to the other end of the field. Botha screamed out, 'That's the last time I'm passing to you until you can drop it further than I can kick it.'

After he kicked his club side's twenty-four points to give them victory in the Cup final he was sitting beside another man on the plane. Botha was a bit surprised that his companion said nothing to him. After a half an hour of total silence he turned around and said, 'I don't think you realise who I am; I'm probably the most famous rugby player in South Africa.'

His companion quietly said: 'I don't think you realise who I am. I play for your team. I'm your first centre.'

PASS THE BUCK

After an injury to his arm Botha was telling a teammate that he had asked his doctor, 'And when my right arm is quite better, will I be able to pass the ball?'

The doctor replied, 'Most certainly – you should be able to pass with ease.'

His teammate replied: 'That's a miracle cure – you could never pass it before.'

PERFECTION PERSONIFIED

The opening line to the fourth Star Wars film was: 'In every generation a new hero is born.' The line could have been written for John Eales. The former Australian captain's nickname is 'Nobody', as in 'nobody's perfect'. Mind you, Eales has often pointed out that nobody has ever called him 'Nobody' to his face.

In 1996 Eales toured Ireland with Australia. There was one heart-stopping moment for him on the tour. He was having his breakfast at the team hotel in Dublin when a message came over the intercom for Eales to contact reception urgently. The message was repeated two further times in tones of ever increasing urgency. Becoming concerned and suspecting a family crisis back home, he identified himself and was quickly given a telephone.

'Mr Eales.'

'Yes.'

'This is your 8 a.m. wake up call ...'

Unlike most rugby players, Eales is renowned for his politeness as much for his prowess in the second row. In 1999 when the team were checking in to their hotel in Perth he said to the lift attendant, 'I'd be grateful if you could let me off at the sixth floor – if it isn't out of your way.'

In a desperate attempt to combat the rugby playing public's perception of Eales as a semi-Godlike figure some of his former international colleagues have started to make jokes about his abilities at golf. They say his first game was a disaster but his golf slowly improved. Eventually he hit a ball in one! Even at his very best he always took two or three lumps with his tee. He bashed his way around the course, cutting divots from the fairways and the greens alike. On his third and final visit he was approached by a stern-faced official who pompously said, 'I am chairman of the green committee ...'

Eales replied, 'I'm delighted to hear that. In fact you're just the man I wanted to see. I had lunch in the restaurant. Those Brussels sprouts weren't fresh.'

His 'friends' claim that such was Eales' desire to find an outlet for his competitive instincts when he retired that he entered a pun contest. He sent in ten different puns in the hope that just one might win.

Sadly, no pun in ten did.

Of course none of these stories are true but there was one memorable time that Eales did face a potential rift with his most illustrious colleague. In 1992 Australia were on tour in Wales. Eales was approached by his prop Ewen McKenzie and asked if he had read the biography of the Scottish rugby captain, David Sole. Ewen proceeded to show him a passage that immediately drained all the blood from the great man's face: 'There is probably nothing I can say about Campo that he hasn't already said himself! Or even as the Wallaby lock John Eales said: "David fell in love with himself ten years ago and has remained faithful ever since!"'

Eales wished the ground would open up and swallow him. He

had playfully mentioned that phrase in the course of a private conversation with Sole as one of the Wallabies' favourite lines. However, he never expected to read it in cold print, with Australia's most iconic figure sitting just a few yards away from him. After the initial fear subsided, Eales decided to deal with the problem head on and venture into the Lion's den to broach his indiscretion directly with Campo. He knocked timidly at Campo's door and after some hesitation eventually mustered up the courage to meekly ask: 'Campo … have … have you seen David Sole's new book?' Much to Eales' relief Campo replied with typical indifference: 'Naaaah, mate, I wouldn't read something like that if you paid me. Who cares?' Eales almost danced with joy and said: 'Good. You're not missing much. It's really terrible.'

It was a much relieved Eales who went to bed that night. The following morning Eales confided his *faux pas* to prop Tony Daly. Daly told him that all his angst was futile. 'You needn't have bothered speaking to Campo about it in the first place. He couldn't be bothered even reading his own book yet, so there's absolutely no way he would even think about reading David Sole's.'

I WANT YOUR SEX

In the 1991 World Cup final, Tim Horan had an even more pressing distraction. In the build up to the final the Australian team had an amazing amount of support from well-wishers, not just the fans who cheered them on their way but many who sent messages to the team hotel. In the lead up to the final the players went into the team room in the hotel from time to time to read the messages. They were incredible: some offered free accommodation at five star hotels, free evenings at massage parlours, free beach holidays, but then came the classic. A woman from Adelaide had faxed in: 'To whoever scores the first try in the final, I will offer you fantastic free sex.' Then she added her phone number.

Once the game started, the first break in the match happened to come from Horan. He was racing down the right-hand side with only Will Carling between himself and the try line. Was he about to get lucky twice in the one moment? He decided to chip through, but the ball went into touch. From the ensuing line-out the Australians managed to pilfer possession, and the forwards drove over the line. The prop, Tony Daly, crashed over the line to score this crucial try, and became an unexpected hero scoring the only try of the match. Tony was a wonderful old-fashioned prop, who won forty-one caps for Australia, but had no future as a male model.

As the whole of Australia watched the game on television the nation's telephone company had its quietest two hours ever. They only took a single call. A lady from Adelaide had rung in to say that she wanted her number changed immediately.

Daly was also believed, though it was never proved, to be responsible for a classic wind-up of David Campese. While the team were staying in a hotel in London a woman approached Campo in the lobby and said: 'Are you John Eales?'

Campo replied, 'No, I'm not.'

'I'm glad. I wouldn't like to see him looking so bad.'

The Italian Job

In 1992 Tim Horan went to visit his good friend Michael Lynagh in Treviso, Italy. The perfect host, Lynagh was anxious to show his guest a good time, and accordingly organised a trip to what is regarded as one of the most stunning cities in the world – Venice. When they arrived, Horan did not have the reaction his friend was expecting: 'Bloody hell, it's been raining a lot here mate, all the roads are flooded.'

'No Tim, this is what Venice is like, it's made up of canals, that's how you get about, all by water.'

'But mate, where do all the cars go?'

BELIEVE IT OR NOT

Like John Eales, Australia's openside George Smith is known as one of the more polite players in rugby. His former coach Rod Macqueen has experienced another side of Smith's character though. Before the first Test against the Lions in 2001, Macqueen was driving from Sydney to Canberra and was ringing the players in his squad individually to let them know whether they were selected or not. The phone was on speaker for ease of driving, with his wife in the passenger seat. Smith was just breaking onto the team at the time and, as is the norm in these situations, he was being constantly wound up by his teammates with all kinds of phone messages purporting to be from the Australian management. When Macqueen rang Smith to tell him the good news that he had made the team he was more than a little surprised by Smith's reaction. The conversation unfolded as follows:

'Hi, George, it's Rod Macqueen.'

'Yeah, sure, f**k off.'

'No George, seriously it really is Rod Macqueen. Congratulations you're in.'

'What a load of bo***cks.'

'George, if you don't believe me please ring any of the other members of the management and check it out.'

Ten minutes later Macqueen took a call. It was Smith. The aggression had melted and was replaced by deference.

'Mr Macqueen, um … it's George Smith here, Mr Macqueen, … um … sir. I'm so, so, so sorry …'

TIME GENTLEMEN PLEASE

The acclaimed New Zealand coach Wayne Smith moved to Italy in 1986 to coach a club called Casale sul Sile. His job required him to work closely with the team manager, Dino Menegazzi. Dino was a little gullible, so an easy target for a wind-up. There is a twelve-hour time difference between Italy and New Zealand and

Smith's new club were going to Rome to play the local team. Smith went into a coffee shop with Menegazzi and started reminiscing about life in New Zealand. Dino was trying to come to grips with the time difference and asked: 'What time would it be in New Zealand now?'

Smith replied: 'Well, it would be about one o'clock tomorrow morning.'

'Nah, it can't be tomorrow down there, really?'

'Well, if I rang my parents they could tell us if we won the game or not.'

Dino scratched his head and looked at Smith and suddenly slammed his fist on the table and said: 'Ring them and if we haven't won, we won't play.'

NAME RECOGNITION

Rudolph Straeuli was a member of the South African World Cup winning squad in 1995 before becoming the ninth Springboks coach since they returned from their enforced isolation in 1992. At the time it was suggested that they had more trainers than Sheikh Mohammed.

Straeuli had problems replicating his success as a player in his role in a tracksuit. He was a bit nervous one day when he had to make a public appearance at a rugby dinner after his team had sustained a bad defeat. His nerves were calmed immediately when an old man came to greet him, giving him a big smile and most enthusiastic handshake, saying, 'It's a great, great pleasure to finally meet you in the flesh. You are a true icon of the game … what's your name again?'

Straeuli was an inevitable casualty after South Africa's inglorious exit from the 2003 World Cup. There was much mirth when details of Straeuli's unconventional training methods emerged after the tournament. His idea of building team morale consisted of getting security guards to force his players down foxholes before dousing them repeatedly with cold water. A new joke was born:

Q: Why did Rudolph Straeuli turn up to the fancy dress party dressed as a pumpkin?

A: He hoped he would turn into a coach at midnight.

It is alleged that part of Straeuli's regime in the infamous Kamp Staaldraad involved having the Springboks train in the nude. In fact, so widespread were the allegations that they were training 'military style' that the South African Major General Mohato Mofokeng felt obliged to state publicly: 'I would like to point out that the South African National Defence Force does not train its people naked, nor, to the best of my knowledge, does any other military organisation. Conditions in the field are not conducive to the naked human form.'

THOSE MAGNIFICENT MEN IN THEIR FLYING MACHINE

Gary Teichmann is one of South Africa's recent great players. He was heading off to play Australia, and just before the plane took off the stewardess asked him if he would like cotton wool or a boiled sweet to combat the pressure difference, 'I'll have the cotton wool,' joked Teichmann. 'I tried the boiled sweets last time but they just kept falling out of my ears.'

THAT HEALING TOUCH

Gareth Edwards sustained an injury playing against England. In the dressing room afterwards Barry John asked him what he was going to do. Gareth said he wasn't too bothered because he had just discovered a wonderful masseuse. Barry asked: 'What is so good about this particular masseuse?'

Edwards innocently replied within earshot of the entire team: 'The beauty of this girl is that she will drop anything for a rugby player.'

Within weeks the masseuse had an expanded practice of almost twenty Welsh internationals.

A less cerebral use of religious language to talk about the great Welsh players is revealed in the following story:

Welsh fan: 'Look there's Barry John.'

English fan: 'So what, he's not the Almighty.'

Welsh fan: 'No, but he's young yet.'

Barry was always in great demand to play in exhibition games. His box office value is illustrated in the story told by Cliff Morgan – there was a large sign outside a rugby ground before a match which read: 'Admission £2. If Barry John Plays – £10.'

Although his nickname was 'the King' the Welsh management were able to ensure that Barry never got too big for his boots. When John Dawes retired from the Welsh captaincy, Barry's name was widely linked to the post. One headline read, 'This is the true crowning of the King.' Barry did not want the extra responsibilities of captaincy and he telephoned the Welsh manager, Clive Rowlands, to air his concerns. Rowlands took the wind out of his sails by saying, 'Don't worry, we haven't even considered you, Barry.'

After an uncharacteristically off day for him a wag was heard saying: 'Barry John can make the ball talk. The problem is, it's saying goodbye.'

Like the majority of Welsh people, Barry is less charitable when it comes to English rugby. One of his favourite questions is: 'What do you call an Englishman holding a bottle of champagne after a Six Nations game?'

'A Waiter.'

THE OLD ONES

In recent years, Barry John has become a central protagonist in the undisputed favourite story of Welsh rugby.

After winning the World Cup in 2003, Clive Woodward was

booked as guest speaker at Upper Cwmtwrch Rugby Club. After delivering his thoughts on the game, the English coach faced questions from the audience. Dai stuck his hand up and asked: 'Mr Woodward, although I never want to see England win, I'm a big admirer of your team and their style of play. Now, I remember the great Welsh sides of the 1970s; tell me, who do you think would win a game between the Welsh greats and your present team?'

Clive thought hard and said: 'David, I loved to watch the Welsh sides of the 1970s. Edwards, J. P. R., Barry John, Gerald Davies … they were brilliant players, winners. They showed how the game should be played. But I have to say, my team – such modern, professional, great athletes. Wilkinson – the best tackling and tactical fly-half ever. Martin Johnson – greatest second row the world's ever seen. I could go through the whole team. I just have to say, I think my boys would win.'

There was uproar in the club, boos, shouts, beer thrown at the stage. When it calmed down, Woodward said: 'Look, David you posed the question. Tell me honestly, who do you think would win?'

Dai looked troubled and said: 'Well, it's not going to be popular here, but you know, Mr Woodward, I think you are right. You would win if we played you tomorrow. You see, all our lads are in their seventies now.'

CHAPTER EIGHT

Ruck and Roll

Tom Humphries has dismissed rugby: 'Rugby people. Can't live with them. Can't shoot them. Mainly can't live with them. Can't afford to live with them. Haven't the bloodlines to live with them. Haven't the patience to love them. Haven't the language skills to live with them. Haven't the desire even. Rugby people have always been college scarves and jutting jaws and silly songs I don't know the words of. C-A-N-N-O-T live with them.' In marked contrast, this chapter celebrates the fans who are the lifeblood of the game.

A RELIGIOUS EXPERIENCE

There was a well-known Holy Ghost priest who coached rugby in Blackrock College who famously said, 'The two most important things in life are the grace of God and a quick heel from the loose – though not necessarily in that order.'

THE STONE AGE

In the 1970s Max Boyce wrote a song about 'blind Irish referees'. It is said that the first settler in Limerick during the stone age spent so much time complaining about rugby referees that his wife said to him in sheer frustration: 'Do something useful. Invent fire.'

The old man and the seat

The All Blacks toured Wales in 1989. They were intrigued by the Welsh fans. Most of their time there the Kiwis were based in the Grand Hotel in Cardiff, as most of the club sides were accessible from there. One day early on in the tour they were walking down the street, getting a breath of fresh air and there was an elderly man sitting on a bench. He recognised the rugby aristocrats immediately and asked: 'Oh boys, who have you got tomorrow?'

'Cardiff,' they replied.

'Cardiff will beat you,' he said. 'Cardiff are a good side. They will beat you.'

Cardiff lost.

A few days later the players met the old man again. 'Who are you playing next?'

'Newport.'

'Newport, good side, tough side, Rodney parade, wide ground, they will beat you.'

Newport lost. The following morning they met the old man and he asked his by now customary question. They replied, 'Neath.'

'Neath are the Welsh champions this year. They will beat you.'

He was wrong again, but the players were too polite to mention this when the familiar ritual was repeated the next time they met him and he confidently predicted, 'Llanelli, at home at Stradley, big crowd. They will beat you.'

Again the All Blacks won. Finally it came to the match they had all been really looking forward to – the Test match against Wales. They again met the old man.

'Who have you got tomorrow?'

'Wales.'

'Oh, Wales, they're bloody crap, you'll beat them.'

HAND-SOME

In fairness to Jim Renwick he could always tell stories against himself. After he dropped a series of passes in an international he was greeted by a Scotland fan who asked Renwick if he could shake hands with him. After the handshake took place the fan said, 'Oh, so you have got hands after all.'

REID ON

According to Jim McCarthy, former Irish centre Paddy Reid should have won a hundred caps for Ireland but he 'only' wore the green jersey six times. Reid is unwilling to blame anybody for his exclusion from the Irish team. His international colleague Jim McCarthy was less reticent and points out that a lot of curious selection decisions have much more to do with politics than with rugby merit – the 'you scratch my back, I'll scratch yours' theory.

'The club rivalry in Limerick is intense. To say there is no love lost between Young Munster and Garryowen is a massive understatement. The incident that best sums this up for me was in 1993, when Liam Hall and I travelled to Dublin to see Young Munster play St Mary's in the decisive match of the AIL. Munsters won. After the game we walked past Johnny Brennan from Munsters and an elderly lady, who I recognised immediately because of her strong connection with the club, though she never had any dealings with me. I turned around and said: "Congratulations, Johnny."

'Johnny told her: "That's Paddy Reid from Garryowen."

'Her reply to this was: "I hates him!"'

OLD RIVALRIES

In 2004 a new chapter in Mick Galwey's life began when he was appointed coach of Shannon, having enjoyed such great success with the club as a player. It was a difficult appointment, particularly given the fierce competition between Shannon and local Limerick rivals Young Munster and Garryowen.

In 2003, immediately after England won the World Cup, BBC Five Live were getting the responses of ecstatic English fans at the match when they stumbled across a sad looking Shannon supporter. He was asked if he was happy with the result.

Fan: 'Not at all. I'm Irish, I'm from Limerick.'

Reporter: 'But would you not support England when Ireland are no longer in the competition?'

Fan: 'No way.'

Reporter: 'Why not?'

Fan: '800 years of oppression.'

Reporter: 'Is there ever any time you would support England?'

Fan: 'If they were playing Young Munster or Garryowen.'

WATER, WATER EVERYWHERE

The Irish swimming fraternity has long been waiting for an Olympic size swimming pool. In 2002 the IRFU began the first phase of its new pitch at Lansdowne Road. Ireland played autumn internationals against both Australia and Argentina during downpours. The pitch was covered in water in many places and barely playable. One swimming fan watching the Argentina match from the stands remarked, 'Congratulations to the IRFU in giving us our first ever 100 metre swimming pool.'

TIME IS PRESSING

Three elderly men, one from Scotland, one from Wales and one from England go into a Church to seek God's help, asking him when their teams would see victory again. The Scotland man asks: 'When will Scotland win the Rugby World Cup?'

A voice booms down from heaven: 'In eight years.'

The Scottish man shakes his head sadly and says: 'I'll be dead by then.'

The Welsh chap is next and he asks: 'When will Wales win the Rugby World Cup?'

A voice booms down from heaven: 'In twelve years.'

The Welsh man shakes his head sadly and says: 'I'll be dead by then.'

The English man asks: 'When will England win the Rugby World Cup?'

God's voice booms down from heaven: 'I'll be dead by then.'

BEAUTY AND THE BEAST

Scottish fans have also been known to tell the odd story against some of the giants of English rugby. This next one is a favourite.

Quasimodo is sitting in his study and once again is feeling depressed about how ugly he is. Looking for some reassurance, he goes in search of Esmeralda. When he finds her, he asks her dejectedly if he really is the ugliest man alive.

Esmeralda sighs and she says, 'Look, why don't you go upstairs and ask the magic mirror who is the ugliest man alive? The mirror will answer your question once and for all.'

About five minutes later, a very pleased looking Quasimodo bounced back down the stairs and gave Esmeralda a great big hug. 'Well, it worked,' Quasimodo beamed, 'But who on earth is Brian Moore?'

HIT HIM HARD

Their definitive story refers to a train journey where an English rugby international, a Scottish international, a spectacular looking blonde and an older lady were sharing a compartment. After several minutes of the trip, the train happened to pass through a dark tunnel and the unmistakable sound of a slap was heard. When they left the tunnel the Englishman had a big red slap mark on his chin.

The blonde thought: 'That horrible English player wanted to touch me and by mistake he must have put his hand on the old lady, who in turn must have slapped his face.'

The older lady thought: 'This dirty English player laid his hands on the blonde and she smacked him.'

The English international thought: 'That bloody Scot put his hand on the blonde and by mistake she hit me.'

The Scot thought: 'I hope there's another tunnel soon so I can smack that stupid English sh*t again.'

UNIMAGINABLE TORTURE

Welsh fans are an equal opportunities lot though. They also enjoy telling stories about the traditional antipathy between Wales and England. One story is about Dai, who was on his way home from the local pub after the Grand Slam win over Ireland in 2005 when he was killed in a road traffic accident. He got up to the pearly gates where St Peter looked him over and enquired of his name – 'Dai Jones'. St Peter got out his book and opened it under J for Jones and said: 'Dear me Dai, it would seem you spent most of your money on beer, and what was left on loose women. To make matters worse, when your mam advised you to get on the straight and narrow you turned that advice down. I'm afraid there's only one place you're going and that is hell.'

So Dai went down, with a heavy heart, looking at the flames of purgatory and listening to the cries of the damned. At the bottom there was a set of double doors which he pushed open and stepped into a blinding light. When he got his bearings he was overcome by disbelief and sheer joy when he realised he was in the Cardiff Millennium Stadium surrounded by tens of thousands of Welsh supporters. At the other end of the stadium there was a huge television screen with the words, 'Next repeat performance starts in four minutes.'

He staggered to the nearest seat with tears on his cheeks saying 'Joy, joy, joy,' whereupon the chap sat next to him leaned over: 'Don't get carried away Dai, we are in hell, it's for all eternity, but the real bad news is they've only got the one DVD and it's England winning the World Cup in 2003.'

CHAPTER NINE

Odd-Shaped Balls

Critics are like eunuchs in a harem: they know how it's done. They've seen it done every day, but they're unable to do it themselves.
Brendan Behan

Rugby and literature have a long history.

It is a little known fact that William Shakespeare, as well as writing, also enjoyed a good game of rugby in his spare time.

So, the team was assembled for practice one Saturday afternoon. It was the middle of winter, and even by English standards it was cold and wet. The pitch was a muddy swamp, and the players decided that they simply couldn't play in those conditions.

They went to the clubhouse for a while, but they soon got bored. And then one of the players had a bright idea: 'Why don't we all go over to William's house?' Shakespeare was doubtful, but they persuaded him, and pretty soon, the whole squad was relaxing in his living room.

True to form as rugby players, they all quickly got drunk, and they came up with an even better idea – to have their rugby practice in the house. As Shakespeare was inebriated he said with uncharacteristic expansiveness: 'Well, it's a big house, after all.' Once they moved some furniture out of the way, they got down to the serious business of practising their sport.

Meanwhile, not far away, the King had just had a great idea for a play, and dispatched a messenger to summon his favourite playwright. When the messenger arrived at the house he could hear this enormous commotion from inside, with shouting and crashes, and he thought Shakespeare must be getting attacked. He braced himself, and crashed through the front door, landing directly in the path of two groups of large, hairy rugby players.

The messenger was pinned to the floor for a while, and he couldn't move. He did manage to free himself momentarily, before getting trapped again, up against a wall. Finally, he escaped, and returned to the palace as quickly as his mangled body would permit.

The king took one look at him, and gasped. 'What happened to you?'

'I think,' said the messenger, 'that I got caught between a ruck and a bard's place.'

This chapter celebrates the relationship between rugby and the media.

A SHOE-IN

When Gerry Murphy was Irish coach he was visited in his home for an interview by popular RTÉ broadcaster Des Cahill. Murphy was on the phone to Michael Bradley when Des arrived, so he ushered his guest into the sitting room before resuming the telephone conversation. Des was waiting for fifteen minutes for the conversation to end and amused himself by looking at the pictures on the wall. He then sat down and for the first time noticed that Murphy had what had once been a beautiful white carpet, only it was covered in mud. This was confirmation, in Des' mind, of the stereotype about rugby players being untidy. Then Murphy joined him. Des was unnerved when he saw Murphy constantly looking down at his guest's shoes. Eventually, Des looked down and was horrified to discover that his shoes were caked in mud. He remembered stepping in a puddle after he had parked his car, but didn't realise that he had accumulated so much muck. It was not the most auspicious start to an interview, destroying his host's exquisite carpet.

THE POOR MOUTH

In November 2014 Bob Geldof went on the *Newsnight* programme to publicise the latest incarnation of his Band Aid project. He gave Irish rugby fans a great laugh when he remarked: 'I came from a poor Irish, not particularly well educated background.' The mirth came from the knowledge that Geldof had attended the greatest bastion of educational and rugby privilege – Blackrock College.

BECAUSE YOU'RE WORTH IT

Ronan O'Gara is now the classic poacher turned gamekeeper as a weekly columnist with *The Examiner* newspaper and as a perceptive and articulate analyst for RTÉ. As a disciple of the John Giles – rather than the Jamie Redknapp – school of analysis, he pulls no punches, and is animated, intense and maintains a flow of relevant information and interpretation.

For media bosses, the temptation to plunder the thoughts of former star players and successful managers and benefit from their judgements is overwhelming, particularly when, like Rog, their name has become the touchstone for mythology. For those personalities who have retired, media involvement affords them the platform to continue their happy addiction to the small and large dramas created by sportsmen when they suspend reality in favour of a private – if heightened – version of it on the pitch. As a television pundit Rog goes much further, never ceasing to inform, enthuse and to entertain, drawing on the depth and authenticity of his experience.

In 2014 O'Gara made his debut as an RTÉ rugby panelist. He

created an immediate impression by joking that the busiest man in Irish rugby was George Hook's make-up artist.

EXPENSIVE

Broadcasters and journalists are not universally loved. Hence the story of the traveller wandering on an island inhabited entirely by cannibals and coming upon a butcher's shop, which specialised in human brains. A sign in the shop read: 'Scientists' brains £20 a lb: economists' brains £40 a lb: philosophers' brains £60 a lb and journalists' brains £200 a lb.' The traveller asked how was it that journalists brains were so expensive. The butcher said: 'It's because you have to kill ten times more journalists to get a pound of brains.'

Many former rugby players have made the transition from player to pundit. They have gone through what Sir Clive Woodward calls the T-Cup, i.e. 'Thinking correctly under pressure.'

MISTAKEN IDENTITY

When Brian Clough was manager of Nottingham Forest a TV crew requested an interview with Gary Charles. Clough sent out a young apprentice who vaguely resembled the full back. None of the panel noticed. Embarrassing.

Sports fans like to think that their sports presenters and analysts have expert knowledge. This was most revealed when a caller to RTÉ Sport was asking about Manchester United only to discover that the call was answered by a doyen of the GAA, the late Seán Óg Ó Ceallacháin. The conversation unfolded as follows:

'Is this Seán Óg?'

'It is indeed.'

'Seán Óg Ó Ceallacháin?'

'The one and the same.'

'Off the radio?'
'That's me!'
'Sure what the f**k would you know about soccer?'

FATHER TED

One of the most important qualities any pundit can have is accessibility: to be able to speak in a way the punters can easily understand. We in Ireland are lucky to have a few masters of this art on RTÉ television. None more so than Ted Walsh. This was illustrated at the Cheltenham Festival after the Champion Hurdle: 'Conor O'Dwyer is as nice a fell as ever pulled his breeches over his knees.'

It is no accident that Ted pops up frequently to intelligently elucidate on both Channel 4 and RTÉ. He is revered by racing fans, and a familiar name to those who know nothing about the sport of kings.

Walsh has rewritten the lexicon of horse racing commentary, popularising such phrases as 'a great lepper', 'bits of chances', 'gutsy buggers' and most famously, 'I rode her mother' – a reference to a horse whose mother he had ridden, lest there be any confusion.

He is not the biggest man in the world but President Truman's comment about size readily springs to mind. 'When it comes to inches, my boy, you should only consider the forehead. Better to have a spare inch between the top of your nose and the hairline than between the ankle and the kneecap.'

STANDING ON THE SHOULDERS OF TV GIANTS

I suppose a lot of people would describe George Hook as a perfectionist. A perfectionist is one who takes great pains – and gives them to everyone else.

Former Liverpool manager, Bill Shankly, said of his full back,

Tommy Smith, that he would raise an argument in a graveyard. The same comment could be made about George Hook.

The job of a rugby pundit, to steal shamelessly from Robert Frost, is to provide what is demanded of a good poem, 'not necessarily a great clarification … but a momentary stay against confusion.' As a television rugby pundit Hook goes much further, never ceasing to inform, infuriate, enthuse, entertain and to extend the boundaries of the English language.

The former Dunfermline player Jim Leishman once said: 'I was the first professional football player to be forced to retire due to public demand.' For his services to the entertainment industry Hook is unlikely to receive such a request from rugby fans. That is not to say he has no critics. One fan said of him: 'We have the problem of spam on the internet and the problem of Hook on TV.'

THE GOOD, THE GLAD AND THE RUGBY

A feature of RTÉ's coverage of the 1991 Rugby World Cup was the way Tony Ward and the much missed Mick 'give it a lash' Doyle slotted smoothly into the roles filled by John Giles and Eamon Dunphy for soccer matches. Like their soccer friends, both men could graphically illustrate their points with the aid of diagrams, and again had the affable Bill O'Herlihy to spark them into new heights of animation.

More recently, a new triumvirate was created with Tom McGurk, George Hook and Brent Pope. The jaw-dropping emotional roller coaster that was the climax of the 2015 Six Nations was a fitting finale for their reign on RTÉ.

What made the dynamic between them so intriguing was that the viewer was never too clear as to whether Tom and George liked each other.

THE RIGHT HOOK

There are, however, a number of pitfalls facing a television pundit. The golden rule is to be careful what you say – not something Hook is noted for. During Harold Macmillan's time as Prime Minister of England, he received a grave message about a diplomatic disaster during a Parliamentary recess. BBC radio reported the event as follows, 'These dismal tidings were delivered to the Prime Minister on the golf course where he was playing a round with Lady Dorothy.' The words read fine in print, but when spoken the sentence took on a very different connotation.

Jimmy Hill asserted that Romania's success in the 1998 World Cup group matches could be attributed in part to their players having dyed their hair blonde. According to Jimmy, it made it easier for them to see their passing options.

COME ON

As an analyst, you have to do your preparation. One of Tony Ward's favourite television appearances dates back to his appearance in 1979 on *A Question of Sport* – the BBC's premier sporting quiz programme. Ward was on Emlyn Hughes' team and Liam Brady was on Gareth Edwards'. Ward was to see Colemanspeak first hand when David Coleman asked Ward's fellow contestant Liam Brady: 'In what sport is a kamen used?' Brady was very surprised to discover that the answer was *hurling*. Coleman had mispronounced 'camán' as 'kamen'.

PUT A CORK IN IT

It is very important for an analyst to know his/her audience. Before the emergence of Tiger Woods, Jack Nicklaus bestrode the world of golf like a colossus. During the height of his powers *The Cork Examiner* sought an interview with him. When their request was put to Jack's PR person he shook his head firmly and said, 'My client would have no interest in being interviewed in a publication that is about nothing but corks.'

Ger Loughnane points to another danger:

'Anthony Daly called me and said that a man came to the door of his shop in Ennis and said, "You shouldn't have said that."

Dalo replied, "What did I say?"

"Well, I don't know. But you shouldn't have said it."

That is the perfect illustration of what people pick up from the paper. That's why I'm glad I always treated the press with the respect they deserved!'

ONE OF A KIND

It is not overstating things to say George Hook's style is unique. Asked why Leinster lost to Perpignan in the Heineken Cup in 2003, he replied: 'It's in Mrs Betton's cookery book – recipe, chicken soup. First catch your chicken; this team has not caught their chicken since this championship started; today that chicken has come home to roost. That's why they're in the manure they're in.' He does not spare people's sensibilities: 'If Frankie Sheahan was playing William Tell his son would have an arrow in his chest and not in his apple.' After Ireland's surprise capitulation to the Scots in 2001 Hook observed: 'Scotland are – I nearly said the nymphomaniacs … of course, I mean the kleptomaniacs of world rugby.'

HOOK AND POPEY

Brent Pope and George Hook are one of the best known double acts in Irish punditry. Pope has other strings to his bow, including fashion design. Asked if he would make clothes for Hook in the light of his generous waistline, Pope replied: 'I've had to make a new category just for George – XXXL.'

Noticing that the Irish captain was carrying a few spare pounds he said: 'Brian O'Driscoll's been going to the same gym as George Hook.'

Hook recognises one of the most important things about the job of an analyst – that they are part of the entertainment business. Hook is one of the people that appreciates that you need a bit of craic as well. This was most evident in March 2005 after Ireland won the Triple Crown by beating Scotland. After the previous game when Ireland beat Italy, George took a dig at Ireland's national treasure Brian O'Driscoll for taking full advantage of his post-match interview on RTÉ to slug out of a highly visible Powerade bottle after every answer. After the Scots game O'Driscoll recruited his centre partner Gordon D'Arcy to join him in slugging out of their Powerade bottles when they were being interviewed by Michael Lyster, presumably as payback for George's little dig. Hook responded with a great stroke. He had prepared his own drink, and when answering questions of his own he was busy slugging out of a 'Hook's Hootch' bottle. Presenter Tom McGurk and Brent Pope were laughing so hard that they had to take an ad break.

REST IN PEACE

Mick Quinn tells the story that George Hook was picking through the frozen turkeys at the local supermarket but he couldn't find one big enough for the family. He asked a passing assistant, 'Do these turkeys get any bigger?'

The assistant replied, 'I'm afraid not, they're dead.'

COUCH POTATOES

Another Mick Quinn story is that Brent Pope, Conor O'Shea and George Hook were arrested for crimes against rugby punditry and sent to Mountjoy. One of the prison guards was a big rugby fan and helped them escape. They escaped to the countryside, but the Gardaí were still on their backs so they hid in a barn and got into some sacks. The Gardaí went in and felt the sack with Pope in it – he went 'Miaow!'

Satisfied they went on to feel the sack with O'Shea in it – he went 'Woof'.

Finally they felt the sack with Hook in it. He shouted: 'Potatoes.'

New kid on the block

After his retirement as a player, Alan Quinlan turned his considerable talents to working with the media. However, not everyone welcomes having a microphone stuck under their face. The legendary Kerry footballer Ger Power was once asked a question in the build-up to a big match. He replied, 'Whatever I said last year, put me down for the same again this time.'

In a world where words are cheap and commentary often passes for 'the boy done great', the only pity is that Quinlan's sharp intelligence and clear descriptions could not be deployed by cross-channel stations for their soccer half-time discussions. Often the brightest thing about their analysis is Jamie Redknapp's jacket. For all that Quinlan clearly enjoys his role as analyst:

'Analysis is not nearly as stressful as management. I haven't been shot yet!'

He is very warm, friendly, affable and good-humoured. He is completely free from the pretension associated with many of his colleagues. Not for him the nickname given to one of his peers, 'The ego has landed.'

Are you right there Michael?

After France's impressive defeat of Ireland and England's unimpressive performance against Wales in the 2004 Six Nations, many pundits predicted that the French would sweep to victory over England in the next round. Not so Ireland's leading rugby commentator, Michael Corcoran. He confidently predicted that 'England will upset the apple tart.'

Another of Michael's gems came the day Ireland claimed the 2004 Triple Crown with a win over Scotland, 'Ronan O'Gara has his boots on the right foot.'

A TONY A-WARD

Some rugby players, like Gavin Henson, are difficult to ignore, but well worth the effort. Others are cut from a different cloth. As a boy growing up in a GAA heartland in Roscommon in the 1970s and worshipping at the shrine of Dermot Earley, neither rugby nor Shakespeare held much appeal for me. All that changed with the emergence of Irish rugby's first superstar, Tony Ward. Those men whom impressionable boys make their heroes carry a heavy burden. What added to his appeal was that his personality was not turned by fame. As Tony O'Reilly said to me in 1993: 'His head was the same size when he won his last cap as it was when he won his first one.'

It was joked that the only advice opposing coaches could give their teams before playing against him was: 'If you can't catch him at least ruffle his hair.' Like many more, I became a rugby addict and he was the ultimate fix.

Mae West famously said, 'Too much of a good thing can be wonderful,' but all this adulation was not to the rugby establishment's taste back then. As Eamon Dunphy wrote at the time 'Dammit, the man was behaving like a bloody soccer player.' What was the Irish selectors' response? They dropped him, of course. Long before Roy Keane and Mick McCarthy in Saipan, Ireland had its first sporting civil war: who should be Ireland's number ten, Tony Ward or Ollie Campbell? It was a debate that divided the rugby nation like never before.

The Good, the Glad and Ollie

No Irish sports star, apart from George Best, filled more news-paper columns than Tony Ward in the 1970s. Ward exploded onto the sporting scene in 1978 when he first played for Ireland. He was already a local hero in Limerick, where he was training to be a PE teacher in Thomond College, because of his displays for one of the city's top teams, Garryowen.

Ward was the unnamed culprit in a story that did the rounds just as he broke onto the Irish team. The story involved two conversations between a Young Munster (Garryowen's great rivals) supporter and his parish priest.

Priest: 'It's a long time since your face has been seen in this sacred house my son. Anyway, we cater for all types here. Can I be of any assistance to you at all?'

Fan: 'I don't know if you can Father. You see this could be a job for the bishop. I am in an awful way. My state of mind is such that all communications with the wife, both verbal and otherwise, have temporarily ceased.'

Priest: 'My son, confession is good for the soul. What is the terrible secret that you bear?'

Fan: 'Father, the truth is … I … I … am in danger of becoming a supporter of the Garryowen team.'

Priest: 'I see. That's bad, in fact, it's very bad.'

Fan: 'I knew you would understand, Father. All my life I thought that rugby consisted of rucks, scrums and line-outs with a few fights thrown in for good measure. Where I come from, shouts of "ahead, ahead" have a different meaning than that employed elsewhere. To be candid, Father, I was happy in my ignorance, but now 'tis all jinking and running, reverse passing and blindside moves. And to make matters worse, Father, I am being entertained by it all. Tell me … do you think I could be losing the faith?'

Priest: 'My son, the ordinary, everyday problems of life – wife-swapping, divorce, drinking – are but minor problems compared to your dilemma. Come back to me tomorrow, I shall have spoken with a higher authority by then.'

After a long night of fretful sleep, the Young Munster supporter returned the next day.

Priest: 'My son you can put your mind to rest. A solution to your problem exists, and where else was it to be found but in religion. Within a year or two the blackguard most responsible for Garryowen's madness and for your unhappy state of mind will be plucked from our midst and transported away. Normality will return.'

Fan: 'But how can I be sure of this?'

Priest: 'My son, the bells of St Mary's will ring out for him … and he will answer their call.'

Shortly afterwards Tony Ward transferred to St Mary's club in Dublin.

OPPORTUNITY KNOCKS

In the history of Irish rugby there has never been a bigger shock than in 1979 when the Irish coach, Noel Murphy, dropped the European Player of the Year Tony Ward for the first Test against Australia and replaced him with the virtually unknown Ollie Campbell. Campbell grabbed the opportunity with both hands and produced a dazzling display and went on to establish himself as one of the top names in world rugby.

Exactly a year later, fate decreed that the three protagonists were brought together again. Murphy was coaching the Lions on their tour to South Africa where his non-Irish players had to get used to his rather unusual instructions such as, 'Spread out in a bunch.'

Campbell was the Lions' chief placekicker as well as out-half. When he sustained an injury it was Murphy who would tell Ward that he was in because Campbell was out. One of South Africa's main newspapers, *The Rand Daily Mail*, made Ward's dramatic summons to the touring party front page news, a tribute to Ward's reputation but also evidence, if any were needed, of the extraordinary importance of rugby in South African society.

With the Ward–Campbell debate still raging, Campbell would have been happier if Ward was back home in Ireland. Not only did Ward play in the first Test, he scored eighteen points – which was then a Lions individual points scoring record in a Test match. Was Campbell to have no escape from this guy?

Ward was a sub to Campbell in the third Test in Port Elizabeth. To his horror, he was in the dressing room before he discovered that he had forgotten his boots. It was too late to retrieve them from the team hotel. His problem was exacerbated by the fact that nobody had a spare pair of boots to lend him. He consoled himself with the thought that he would probably not need them.

The seating arrangements for the subs that day were bizarre to say the least. They were to sit on the very top row of the stadium. As the match began Ward was making the long journey up countless flights of stairs with John Robbie when he heard somebody shouting for him. Campbell was injured in the very first moments of the match and was pumping blood. He still has a small scar on his face as a 'souvenir'. It looked like Ward would have to play!

It was panic stations all round. John Robbie got a pair of boots from a ballboy for Ward to wear. A size nine, they were too big for him, but an even more serious problem was that the studs were moulded. The pitch was waterlogged that day and even if they had been the right size they would have been a disaster in the conditions, but they were all he had at the time. Ultimately Campbell was able to play on but he jokes about a lost opportunity to scuttle his rival's career. If only he had known about Ward's predicament, he would have been straight off the pitch. It would have been Wardy's ultimate nightmare and his reputation would have been destroyed at a stroke.

THE UNUSUAL SUSPECTS

One of the other players on the tour with Ward was the Welsh centre Ray Gravell. They shared a few good moments on the tour. Ray was famous for singing Welsh nationalistic songs before big games. One day he confided to Ward: 'Tony, I can't stop singing The Green, Green Grass of home.'

Ward replied: 'That sounds like Tom Jones syndrome.'

'Is it common?'

'It's not unusual.'

FLIPPER AND THE COMANCHERO

Ward immediately struck up a close friendship with Scotland's Jim Renwick when he played for the Lions. On the tour Ward nearly lost his life. He had been relaxing with the squad at the Umhalgna Rocks Indian Ocean resort north of Durban and went for a swim. He is a poor swimmer, and the undertow was very strong and carried him out until he was literally out of his depth. He started shouting and his fellow Irish international John O'Driscoll, who is a very strong swimmer, and the lifeguard rescued him. Having just had the most scary experience of his life Ward might have expected sympathy, but Renwick's response was to immediately christen him, 'Flipper'.

Jim's nickname was 'the Comanchero' after the song of the same name. The following season Ireland were to play Scotland in Murrayfield. Ward arranged to have a telegram sent to Renwick in the team hotel on the day before the match which read: 'Comanchero beware. Flipper's in town.'

About an hour before the game the teams went out to inspect the pitch. Part of the psychological warfare that goes on before a major international is that a player seldom makes eye contact with the opposition. They keep their head down and count the daisies rather than look an opposing player in the face. The Irish were coming out of the tunnel with the Scottish players, but neither

Renwick nor Ward could stop themselves from looking at each other out of the corner of their eye. Ward smiled feeling he had one up on him because of the telegram. When they went back inside after the pitch inspection, the Secretary of the Scottish Rugby Football Union came into the Irish dressing room saying: 'Telegram for Mr Ward.' It read simply: 'Flipper shut your zipper. The Comanchero!'

LIFE AT NUMBER TEN

Tony's passion for the game is as strong today as in his playing days. I saw this at first hand watching him filling in a credit card application form. When it came to the question that asked: 'What is your position in the company?' He answered: 'Out-half.'

DOYLER

The late Mick Doyle famously coached Ireland to the Triple Crown in 1985. He was a star player for both Ireland and the Lions. On the Lions tour Doyler was as well known for his off-field exploits as for those on it, particularly in exposing the gap between 'The Wreckers' and 'The Kippers', the latter being those who liked to get an early night and the former those who chose to get as late a night as possible.

Although he played on his 'give it a lash' image, he was a very shrewd coach. Before getting the Ireland job he was coach of Leinster. The province played Romania when they toured Ireland in 1980. The home side arrived at the ground well over an hour before the game. Players thought they had mistimed the arrival. The previous week Romania had hammered Munster, and Doyler had noticed in the lead up to the match the Romanian players were constantly in and out of the toilet. Being the cute Kerryman that he was, Doyler gave a newspaper and a match programme to each of the Leinster substitutes and told them to lock themselves in the toilets until the game began. Leinster demolished the Romanians in the match. The next day the phrase used in the newspapers was, 'The Romanians were strangely heavy and leaden-footed.' Was it any surprise?

This drowning man

Phil O'Callaghan has a clear memory of Doyler:

'We had a magnificent team, brilliantly led by Tom Kiernan, that toured Australia, and we stopped off in Hawaii. At one stage we were standing at the side of a swimming pool. I had my back to the deep end and was pushed in by Mick Doyle. I was not able to swim and went under. The guys thought I was faking it when I didn't surface. I owe a great debt of gratitude to Terry Moore who dived in and lifted me out of the water long enough to give me the air I needed before I went down again. The great Dr Jerry Walsh found the pole for cleaning the pool and extended it to me and I eventually hauled myself out of the pool. I asked Jerry later why he had not dived in. He said: "Why ruin the tour by having both of us drown?"'

Tougher than the rest

One night before a big match for Leinster Terry Kennedy, Ronan Kearney and Mike Gibson came in at an ungodly hour after a night on the town. The Leinster coach at the time, Mick Doyle, decided to crack the whip. The next morning the three players were summoned to attend Doyler's room at 11 a.m. Doyle was sharing with Ken Ging. The problem was that the previous night the selectors had had a right old party themselves, and the room was covered with empty bottles. Ging was told to tidy up and he hid them under a chair in the corner.

The three lads arrived at the appointed hour and Ollie Campbell, who was captain that year, was asked to attend. Doyler proceeded to tear into the three miscreants, using every cliché in the book about how they were a disgrace to Leinster and how they had let themselves down. Ollie was a very uncomfortable witness to this tirade. He pulled out the chair from the corner to sit down and the bottles went spinning all over the floor. Terry Kennedy and Mike Gibson burst out laughing and said, 'F**k off Doyler.'

LEGAL DISPUTE

For his part, Gibson featured in one of the stories told to me by Mick Doyle. Jonathan Davies, Gibson and Rob Andrew were all in Saudi Arabia, sharing a smuggled crate of booze when, all of a sudden, Saudi police rushed in and arrested them. The mere possession of alcohol is a severe offence in Saudi Arabia, so for the terrible crime of actually being caught consuming the booze, they were all sentenced to death. However, after many months and with the help of very good lawyers, they were able to successfully appeal their sentences down to life imprisonment.

By a stroke of luck, it was a Saudi national holiday the day after their trial finished, and the extremely benevolent Sheikh decided they could be released after receiving just twenty lashes each of the whip. As they were preparing for the punishment, the Sheikh announced: 'It's my first wife's birthday today, and she has asked me to allow each of you one wish before your whipping.'

Jonathan Davies was first in line. He thought for a while and then said: 'Please tie a pillow to my back.' This was done, but the pillow only lasted ten lashes before the whip went through. When the punishment was done he had to be carried away bleeding and crying with pain.

Rob Andrew was next up. After watching the Welshman in horror he said smugly: 'Please fix two pillows to my back.' But even two pillows could only take fifteen lashes before the whip went through again and the Englishman was soon led away whimpering loudly.

Gibson was the last one up, but before he could say anything, the Sheikh turned to him and said: 'You are from the most beautiful part of the world and your culture is one of the finest. For this, you may have two wishes.' 'Thank you, your Most Royal and Merciful highness,' Gibson replied. 'In recognition of your kindness, my first wish is that you give me not twenty, but one hundred lashes.' 'Not only are you an honourable, handsome and powerful man, you are also very brave,' the Sheikh said with an admiring look on his face. 'If one hundred lashes is what you desire, then so be it. And your second wish, what is it to be?' the Sheikh asked.

'Tie the Englishman to my back.'

BESTSELLER

After his career as Irish coach ended Mick Doyle wrote his autobiography, which was described by one observer as 'a good love guide'. He rang up the then Taoiseach Charlie Haughey to see would he be willing to launch the book. Haughey asked him what it was about. Doyle said twenty per cent was about rugby and eighty per cent was pornography. Haughey said, 'You got the balance just right!' Charlie opened his speech on the night by saying, 'I always like people who expose themselves in public.'

At a book signing a few men arrived dressed up as nuns. One of the scenes in the book relates how Doyler was caught in a state of undress by a nun after performing the 'marital act'.

Some time later Doyler was doing a book signing in O'Mahony's bookshop in Limerick. Former Taoiseach Garret FitzGerald had been there the night before promoting his autobiography. In the front window they had photographs of both Doyle and FitzGerald. As he prepared for his signing, Doyler noticed a religious brother in his white collar walking up and down past the shop shouting 'Get that bast**d off the window.' One of the shop assistants went out and asked him, 'What's wrong with Mick Doyle?'

'Nothing. He's a grand fella. It's that other so-and-so that I can't stand.'

There was some very hostile reactions to the book, as it recounted some of his sexual conquests in vivid detail. Doyle claimed that the best story he heard about his book was of two women discussing it. One said: 'I can't understand how anybody wrote a book like that while they were still alive!'

There was some suggestion that Doyler must have added to some of the stories about his off the field activities in his autobiography. One of the players who knew him best, Jim Glennon, disagreed. His feeling was that they were probably slightly understated!

MAKING AN ASS OF YOURSELF

Doyler also explained the duty of the rugby analyst to me when he told me the parable of the donkey and the bridge.

A man and his son were bringing their donkey to the fair. The man was walking with the donkey and his son was up on the animal's back. A passerby said: 'Isn't it a disgrace to see that poor man walking and the young fella up on the donkey having an easy time. He should walk and let his poor father have a rest.'

So the boy dismounted and the father took his place. A mile later they met another man who said: 'Isn't it a disgrace to see that man sitting up on the donkey's back and his poor son walking. He should let his son get up on the donkey with him.' When the man heard this he instructed his son to get up on the donkey's back with him. After they travelled another mile they met a woman. She said: 'Isn't it a disgrace to see those two heavy men up on that poor little donkey's back. They should get down off him and carry the donkey for a change.' The father and son dismounted, got a pole from the side of the road and tied the donkey to it and they carried him across their shoulders. Then disaster struck. Tragically, the donkey fell into the river as they walked over the bridge and drowned.

The moral of the story is that if you are a rugby analyst and you are trying to please everyone you might as well kiss your ass goodbye.

L-ANKER

Doyler had many stories about his players from that team, notably his full back Hugo MacNeill, who was famous for his good looks.

'One evening Hugo took his blind date to the carnival. "What would you like to do?" he asked.

"I want to get weighed," she said.

They strolled over to the weight guesser. He guessed 130 pounds. She was delighted and was given a teddy bear as her prize. Next the couple went onto the ferris wheel. When the ride was over, Hugo asked her what she would like to do. "I want to get weighed," she said.

Back to the weight guesser they went. Again Hugo guessed correctly and won another teddy bear.

The couple walked around the carnival and again he asked her where she would like to go. "I want to get weighed," she responded. By this time, Hugo figured he should cut his losses and dropped her home.

Her flatmate, Laura, asked her about the blind date.

Rachel responded, "Oh, Waura, it was wousy."'

CURVY

In fairness Doyler told more stories against himself than anybody else. He frequently joked about his weight: 'I have flabby thighs, but fortunately my stomach covers them.

'We have a tradition of walking in our family to fight the battle of the bulge. My uncle started walking five miles a day when he was sixty. He's ninety-seven now and we don't know where the f**k he is.

'I like long walks myself, especially when they are taken by people who annoy me.'

GONE BUT NEVER TO BE FORGOTTEN

Every meeting with Doyler was memorable. My final encounter with him was a few months before his tragic death. He had just been listening to a report that Greece might not be able to finish building all the events for the summer's Olympics. Doyler joked that as a result, the 2004 triathlon would combine running, swimming and pouring concrete.

However, what really had put a spring in his step was that he had heard a joke that morning about the visit of President George Bush to England.

While visiting England, Bush was invited to tea with the Queen in Buckingham Palace. With an eye to the forthcoming Presidential election Bush was keen to pick her brain and asked her about her leadership philosophy. She told him it was to surround herself with intelligent people. Bush asked how she knew if they were intelligent.

'I do so by asking them the right questions,' said the Queen. 'Let me show you.'

Bush watched as the Queen phoned Tony Blair and said: 'Mr Prime Minister, may I ask you a question? Your mother has a child, and your father has a child, and it is not your brother or sister. Who is it?'

Blair replies, 'It's me, ma'am.'

'Correct. Thank you and goodbye, sir,' said the Queen. She hung up and said: 'You see what I mean, Mr Bush?'

Bush nods: 'Yes ma'am. Thanks a lot. I'll definitely be using that.'

Bush, upon returning to Washington, decided he'd better put his administration to his test. Bush summoned his vice president, Dick Cheney, to the oval office and said, 'I wonder if you can answer a question for me.'

'Why, of course, sir. What's on your mind?'

Bush posed the question: 'Uh, your mother has a child, and your father has a child and it is not your brother or your sister. Who is it?'

Cheney scratched his head, 'I do not know, sir. That's too tough for me. You will need the most intelligent member of your administration for that.'

That evening Colin Powell was summoned to the West Wing. The president asked: 'Uh, your mother has a child, and your father has a child and it is not your brother or your sister. Who is it?'

'It is me, Mr President.'

President Bush hung his head. 'You dumb sh*t. You're so wrong. Of course it's not you – it's Tony Blair.'

No Pat on the back

Doyler's legacy continues in RTÉ television in the unlikely form of Pat Spillane:

'Kenneth Tynan said: "A critic is a man who knows the way but can't drive the car." The biggest influence on my style as a pundit was Mick Doyle, who died so tragically in a car accident. Mick was a great friend of mine. Doyler and Mandy were at my wedding and it was probably Doyler more than anyone else who encouraged me to become a sports pundit. Mick used to come to Kerry on holidays and bought a house there and we became good friends. Unconsciously, I suppose, I imitated Doyle's style on the telly as I have a lot of Doyler's traits in me.

'I was at the game in March when Ireland beat Scotland to win the Triple Crown in 2004. What I remember most forcefully from the game was listening to 'Ireland's Call' before the match. It wouldn't exactly psych up a person to go into battle.

'The night before the game Mick Doyle was asked what it was he most disliked about rugby today. He replied: "I'm not sure whether it's Brian O'Driscoll's hair or 'Ireland's Call'."'

The Kerryman

Mick Galwey feels that his training as a Gaelic footballer was a big help to his rugby career, primarily in terms of having an eye for the ball. However, he feels that the primary benefit of his association with Kerry was not on the playing field. Former Irish rugby coach Mick Doyle's first love was the GAA, though when he began his secondary education as a boarder in Newbridge College rugby exploded into his life. He continued to trenchantly air his views about the state of Irish rugby through his weekly column in *The Sunday Independent*. His criticism was such that Moss Keane once said to him, 'Thanks be to Jaysus I don't play any more. Otherwise I'd be afraid to open the paper on a Sunday because of what you'd say about me.'

Gaillimh never incurred Doyler's wrath, and contends that the best help his Kerry roots have been to his rugby reputation is that Mick Doyle never wrote anything critical about him – unlike other second row forwards that one could think of.

The road not taken

Another well-known Kerryman to play rugby was one of Ireland's best-loved journalists, Con Houlihan, who lined out for his beloved Castleisland. He took his fair share of heavy tackles and recalled his career, 'I never got capped for Ireland, but I got kneecapped for Castleisland.'

Love and marriage

One of the biggest stars on Mick Doyle's Triple Crown winning team in 1985 was Philip Matthews – now a celebrated analyst with the BBC. He made his international debut against Australia in 1984. That day was to prove the most significant in Matthews' life, because at the post-match reception he met Lisa Flynn, daughter of former great Kevin Flynn – the woman who would become his wife. Love stories begin in Irish rugby! Matthews cringes at the memory, as he was in a bit of a drunken haze at the time. He remembers he was also introduced to Kevin that night and doubts if his future father-in-law was very impressed. He is pretty sure that Kevin didn't want his daughter falling for a drunken yob. He asked Lisa to be his guest at the dinner after their next home international against England. He almost forgot about it, but the rest of the lads reminded him and told him that, as a former chairman of the Irish selectors, it would not be a good idea to let the man's daughter down!

ON A SUNDAY MORNING SIDEWALK

Shay Deering was one of the most loved men in Irish rugby. On the 1976 tour to New Zealand Deero went out partying with Stewart McKinney after a big match on Saturday and came down the next morning for breakfast. The former *Irish Times* correspondent Ned van Esbeck misread the situation when he met the dishevelled pair outside the dining room. His comment was: 'Some things never change. Seamus up early for Mass and McKinney just back from a night on the tiles.'

QUINN'S WORTH

Mick Quinn has also made the transition from ex player to pundit with Newstalk. He sometimes adds a little colour by drawing on quotes from the world of soccer. His top five are:

No matter how much you're expecting it. It's still unexpected when it comes.
– Jason McAteer upon learning that he had just been sacked as Tranmere's assistant boss.

It's a great profession being a referee. They are never wrong.
– Arsene Wenger.

I haven't seen the lad but he comes highly recommended by my greengrocer.
– Brian Clough on signing Nigel Jemson.

Anyone who uses the word 'quintessentially' in a half-time talk is talking crap.
– Mick McCarthy after a contribution from Niall Quinn.

I always enjoy the summer. You can't lose any matches.
– Former Liverpool manager Roy Evans.

SELF ANALYSIS

When I asked the mighty Quinn about his role in the media he replied: 'How do I sum up my life as an analyst? I can only quote the wise words of David Brent, star of *The Office*: "Accept that some days you are the pigeon, and some days you are the statue."'

WORDS TO THE WISE

I asked the bold Mick for five pieces of wisdom for this book. They came as follows:

Hedgehogs. Why can't they just share the hedge?

I hate people who quote me, and you can quote me on that.

People say I am a compulsive liar and that's the truth.

I am making a new series about Mayo footballers. It's called *Footballers' Husbands*.

Q: Why is it getting harder to buy Advent calendars?

A: Because their days are numbered.

LAST WILL AND TESTAMENT

I moved on to ask Mick what he thought his legacy to be:

'What does posterity need me for? Nothing. But what would I like said about me at my funeral? I'd like someone to say, 'Look! He's moving!"'

Should've gone to Specsavers

Bill Lothian, rugby correspondent with the *Edinburgh Evening News* once stated that, 'The front row is an immensely technical place where brain and brawn collide; it is one which has fascinated me since I played with a prop whose shorts caught fire during a game as a consequence of carrying a light for his half-time fag.'

One of Bill's great heroes was 'Mighty Mouse', Ian McLauchlan. The diminutive McLauchlan was capped as a loosehead prop forty-three times and captained Scotland in nineteen major internationals. There is a famous picture of Ian on tour with the Lions in 1974, lifting one huge South African prop clean off the ground in a scrummage.

Mighty Mouse was not always receptive to referees who made bad decisions which cost Scotland. When one disallowed a try which the Scots felt was legitimate, Ian was asked for his verdict afterwards, 'Far be it for me to criticise the referee, but I saw him after the match and he was heading straight to the optician's. Guess who he bumped into on the way? Everyone.'

Mighty Mouse

Mighty Mouse was at the centre of a revealing incident on the 1974 Lions tour. He asked Stewart McKinney which was the greatest honour, to play for Ireland or the Lions. Stewart thought for ten seconds before saying Ireland. Ian slapped him on the face: 'Did I say the wrong thing?' asked McKinney.

'No, you gave the right answer.'

'Then why did you slap me?'

'Because it took you ten seconds to find it,' replied McLauchlan.

Today forwards go in for fancy handling, but in the old days a forward's job was to get the ball and give it straight to the backs. That is why Mighty Mouse was terrified when someone passed to him in an international at Twickenham, 'Jaysus, there was I, in the middle of Twickenham with 60,000 looking on, and with this thing in me hands.'

In 1971 Scotland played England twice on consecutive Saturdays. In the first game at Twickenham the tactics in the front row were very 'robust'. One of the England forwards complained bitterly to McLauchlan, 'We don't play like that down here.'

Mighty Mouse retorted, 'Well, sonny boy, you've got a week to find out just how to do it.'

His attitude to the game was most starkly revealed when he was acting as summariser for BBC television when Scotland played Ireland in Murrayfield. The Irish lock Neil Francis swung a punch, but missed his intended target. Ian was concerned, but not about the violence. With millions of viewers watching he warned Francis that he was in serious danger of getting the name of a softie because 'there isn't much point in having a go at somebody unless you make sure that you connect.'

Franno has gone on to become one of the most colourful writers about rugby in Ireland. A typical Neil Francis opening line is:

'In terms of universal deceit, telling the truth is a revolutionary act.' (George Orwell)

IT TAKES A THIEF

Victor Costello has experienced Franno's wrath at first hand:

'The tradition is that when you win your first cap everybody buys you a drink. When I won mine I took a knock on the head and had to go to bed for a while, but I met up with the lads later on that night. When I got back to the hotel I was starving. The problem was that it was three in the morning. I asked the receptionist how I might get some food. She told me that I could ring out for pizza, but it was very slow.

Just after I dialled in my order, a delivery guy walked into the room with a pizza. I was rooming with Neil Francis at the time and I quickly realised that the pizza was for him. I pretended it was for me though, and I brought it to the tea room and scoffed it all down. When I went up to our room Franno was watching television. I was absolutely stuffed but I pretended to be starving and asked him how I could get some food. He told me that I could ring out for pizza but he told me not to bother because it was so slow and that he had rang for a pizza over an hour earlier and it still hadn't arrived. I was very sympathetic and I asked him if he would mind waking me up and giving me a slice when his pizza finally arrived. He generously agreed.

'The only problem was that the next morning he found the pizza box in the tea room and he discovered it was me that ate it. He actually was really annoyed, and to this day he has never forgiven me! In fact whenever he writes about me in his column he will never call me Victor – he insists on referring to me as "the Pizza robber".'

THE VOICE

In the rugby world the doyen of all media people was the late Bill McLaren. Bill McLaren's own rugby playing career with Hawick came to an abrupt end in October 1948 when it emerged that he had contracted tuberculosis of the lungs. As a player McLaren was no shrinking violet. His father delighted in recalling an incident when he was watching his son play against Kelso and was seated beside a large farmer supporting Kelso. Outraged by Bill's robust tactics, the farmer referred to 'that big, dirty bugger, McLaren.' Discretion was the better part of valour and Bill's dad decided that was not the right moment to profess his connection with his son.

NO GEORGE CLOONEY

Bill was well able to tell stories against himself. During the 1987 World Cup he introduced his wife, Bette, to leading rugby administrator, Syd Millar. Syd took one look at Bill, one at Bette and then said, 'Ah, Jaysus, Bette, you could have done a hell of a sight better!'

UNDRESSED FOR THE OCCASION

Bill's favourite quip was one of Mick Quinn's. Whenever a young lady is introduced to him he says, 'Ah, hello again. How are you? I didn't recognise you with your clothes on!'

LOVELY LIMERICK

Loved universally wherever he travelled, Bill was a big hit when he travelled to the home of Irish rugby, Limerick, for the Terry Wogan Golf Classic in 1991. The only problem was that when Terry Wogan made his speech to the crowd, he said that being a Scot, Bill McLaren was unlikely to throw his ball to the crowd at the end of the round!

WORDSMITH

McLaren's ode to a young Boroughmuir prop forward with a muscular physique was, 'He's built like a young bull.' He also had a nice euphemism for kicking a player, 'Illegal use of the boot.'

ENTHUSIASM GONE MAD

Medics were consulted when before the 2003 World Cup Bill was heard to say: 'Scotland for the World Cup.' Their diagnosis was a nasty case of 'premature e-jock-ulation'.

WEE MEN

When asked by this writer to tell his favourite story, Bill recalled the build-up to a Scotland vs Wales match in 1962. Hugh Ferns McLeod was reluctant to lead the Scottish team at first, as he wanted to focus on his job as prop, but once he was persuaded to do so by a Scottish selector, Alf Wilson, he wanted to do it properly. As Hugh was giving his team talk he noticed the forwards weren't paying attention and were talking amongst themselves. He was five foot ten inches, and he walked up to the forwards who were all towering over him. Undaunted, Hugh said, 'Come here ma wee disciples.' When they all gathered around he continued, 'Now, ah want tae tel ee that ah've been asked ti lead this pack tomorrow, that ah'm no very keen on the job, but that's what ah'm going to do and if any of you lot want to be pack leader, just let me know and ah'll put a word in for you at the right place. The next one who opens his trap ah'll bring my boot right at his arse.'

One of the Anglo–Scots in the group said, 'Well, I didn't understand a word of that but it all sounded damn impressive.' They listened, and the next day beat Wales off the park – their first win in Wales for twenty-five years, and their first win in Cardiff for thirty-five years.

LITTLE AND LARGE

Bill also told the story of another of Hugh's motivational speeches. It came the following year before Scotland played France in Paris. Hugh went up to his fellow forward Frans ten Bos and said, 'Frans, ye think ye're a guid forrit but really ye're jist a big lump o' potted meat. Ah'm going ti tell ye somethin. If ah was half yer size ah'd pick up the first two Frenchmen that looked at me the morn and ah'chuck them right over the bloody stand.' The next day Frans had the game of his life and Scotland won by 11 points to 6.

I can't conceive

Bill claimed that one of his most embarrassing moments came before commentating on England vs France in 1983. France had two locks new to the championship in Jean Condom and Jean-Charles Orso. While it was a relief to discover that Condom pronounced his name *Condong*, Bill joked that the embarrassment came in discovering what a condom was.

The voice was delighted though that he never made a *faux pas* comparable to that of his BBC colleagues, Peter West and Bob Wilson. Commentating on Wimbledon West said: 'Bjorn Borg, the top wanking Swede.' Wilson's misfortune was to say, 'News just through from Elland Road that Joe Jordan has just p***ed a late fatness test.'

Come dine with Fran

In 1973 France played England in Twickenham. Before the match, McLaren was asked on *Grandstand*'s preview what he thought of Fran Cotton. Bill replied, 'I haven't seen the big lad play yet but I had dinner with the England party last night and I saw Fran deal with a five course dinner. He was very impressive indeed.'

Held back at school

Although he was the voice of rugby, Bill's other profession was as a PE teacher at Drumlanrig St Cuthbert's primary school in Hawick. His most famous pupil was former Scottish and Lions centre, Jim Renwick. When Bill retired from teaching in 1988 Jim was invited to make the presentation. The event was covered by BBC television. The interviewer asked Jim, 'Do you think that you would have gained fifty-two caps if you had not been coached by Bill McLaren?'

Jim paused theatrically, 'I think I would have got seventy caps if I hadn't been coached by Bill McLaren.'

BON VOYAGE

In 1984 Scotland toured Romania. At the time things were pretty bleak behind the Iron Curtain, and the Scottish team were in dire straits food-wise. Bill McLaren was due to travel out to see them play and Renwick contacted him begging him to bring out food to the Scottish team. Bill nervously packed tins of sausages, beans and corned beef, as well as Mars bars in his bag knowing that he would be in serious trouble if the custom authorities in Romania – a group of men not known for their understanding or sympathy – caught him out. When he got to Bucharest airport, Bill was approached by two burly security men who would have scared Hannibal Lecter and told to step aside. Bill could practically hear the clang of the cell door closing. He was already visualising himself in a starring role in scenes from the film *Midnight Express*.

A long time passed as Bill waited in terror. Then it emerged that the problem was not his luggage but his passport. His passport described him as a teacher of physical education, whereas in the document he filled in on the flight over he had described himself as a television commentator. Eventually the confusion was resolved, and Bill's frayed nerves were finally soothed once he got outside the airport. He went straight to the Scottish team's hotel and gave Jim the food. The next day Jim thanked him for the food. When Bill asked if it had been well received Jim replied, 'Oh it was brilliant. They were so hungry they ate the tins as well.'

THE BIGGER THEY ARE …

Before Scotland took on the might of the English pack, Doddie Weir suggested to Jim that 'The bigger they are the harder they fall.'

Renwick replied, 'Wrong. The bigger they are the harder they hit you.'

Jim often had a sarcastic edge. After Bruce Hay, who was not known for his speed, scored a try for Scotland he said, 'That's the first time I've seen a try scored live and in slow motion at the same time.'

HAYMAKER

Renwick was not the only one to come down hard on the Lions player. The Duke of Edinburgh was presented to Hay before a match and said, 'And which lamp post did you bump into?'

SHOCK MOVE

During the 2003 World Cup, the media never missed the opportunity to put the boot into the English team. 'Lugergate' afforded them the perfect opportunity. England's Dan Luger came on as a substitute and played against Samoa as a sixteenth man without another English player leaving the pitch for a brief period before the officials spotted the transgression. *The Sydney Morning Herald* saw the humour in the situation and began its preview of England's next game with a nice little barb: 'Clive Woodward sprang a surprise yesterday by naming only fifteen players in his team to meet Uruguay in Brisbane on Sunday.'

However, the most noteworthy piece of English baiting during the tournament came from Australian journalist Mike Gibson. He wrote: 'England boring? We're talking about a nation of people whose idea of risk-taking is to buy a ticket in the pools. Whose idea of excitement is to join a queue. This is a country where the liveliest sporting action is found under the staircase at Buckingham Palace.'

DOSH AND BECKS

What people sometimes underestimate about Jonny Wilkinson is his intelligence. In the run up to the 2003 World Cup, the glamour boys of English rugby and English football, Wilkinson and David

Beckham respectively, were in a TV campaign for a sporting company. Wilkinson was shown teaching Becks to strike a rugby ball. On the eve of their opening match in the rugby World Cup, England faced Turkey to decide who would compete in the European football championships in 2004. England's best chance in the game came when they were awarded a penalty. Beckham stepped up to take it but blazed the ball high over the bar. Afterwards Wilkinson joked, 'David's been spending too much time with me.'

THE PRINCE OF WALES

This is the great stuff. Phil Bennett covering, chased by Alistair Scown. Brilliant, oh that's brilliant! John Williams, Bryan Williams ... Pullin ... John Dawes, great dummy ... To David, Tom David, the half-way line! ... Brilliant by Quinnell! This is Gareth Edwards! A dramatic start! WHAT A SCORE!!

Cliff Morgan's commentary of the most talked about try in one of the most talked about games of all time, when the Barbarians beat New Zealand 23–11 on 27 January 1973. That score is now universally known as 'that try' in the same way as Elizabeth Hurley's revealing dress for the Premier of *Four Weddings and a Funeral* is known simply as 'that dress'. It is right and fitting that it was set up by the Welsh wizard, Phil 'Benny' Bennett. He may not have been as beautiful as Elizabeth Hurley, but nobody has ever made a more determined attempt to make rugby the beautiful game. His sidestep bamboozled the 1973 All Blacks in that famous try for Gareth Edwards. If you want to sell the game of rugby you could not do it better than to show that game again and again.

BIG WILLIE

In 1977 Bennett became only the second Welshman to captain a Lions tour, having captained Wales throughout the season. On a tour the difference between failure and success can be so thin you can hardly see it. That rain-drenched tour was a massive disappointment for the Northern hemisphere side, but nonetheless Phil finished top scorer with 125 points, playing fifteen of twenty-six games and all four Tests. As if he didn't have enough problems on the field, Phil also had to contend with a media circus.

As captain of the Lions team, Bennett needed players willing to shed blood for the cause. He found one in Willie Duggan. During one match Willie was so battered and bloodied that he went off for stitches just before half-time. When the rest of the team came into the dressing room they saw him sitting there with a fag in one hand and a bottle of beer in the other as they stitched up his face. 'Bad luck, Willie. Well played,' Bennett said. 'What do you mean?' Willie demanded. 'As soon as the f**ker sorts my face out I'll be back on.'

On the tour, Willie played for the Lions against a Maori team in a very physical contest. At one stage he was trapped at the bottom of a ruck when a few players kicked him on his head. True to form he got up and carried on. After the game, Bennett asked him if he remembered the pounding on his head. His reply was vintage Dugganesque: 'I do. I heard it.'

THE HAND OF HISTORY ON HIS SHOULDER

Of course, Benny's speech had to include a reference to the traditional Anglo–Welsh rivalry. His story was a reworking of the biblical story of the book of Genesis. In the beginning, the Lord God almighty turned to his best, the archangel Gabriel, and said: 'Gabby, today I am going to create a beautiful part of the earth and I will call it Wales. I will make it a country of breathtaking blue lakes, rich green forests and dark beautiful mountains, which from time to time will be snow-covered. I will give it clear, swift rivers, which will overflow with salmon and trout. The land shall be lush and fertile, on which the people can raise cattle and grow their food, as well as being rich with precious metals and stones that will be sought the world over.

'Underneath the land I shall lay rich seams of coal for the inhabitants to mine. Around the coast, I will make some of the most beautiful areas in the world. Golden sandy beaches and cliffs that will attract all matter of wildlife, with lots of islands that will be like a paradise to all who visit them. In the deep blue waters around the shores, there will be an abundance of sea life. The people who live there will be called the Welsh and will be the friendliest people on earth.'

'Excuse me sir,' interrupted the archangel Gabriel, 'don't you think you're being a bit too generous to these Welsh?'

'Don't talk rubbish,' replied the Lord. 'Wait till you see the neighbours I'm giving them.'

THE FAB FOUR

It may be difficult to believe, but sometimes TV pundits get their phrasing wrong or mix up their metaphors. The result is often memorable for the viewer. I am happy to report that RTÉ's rugby coverage has provided a few classics in this respect. My top four are:

1. 'The coach couldn't give directions to the team hotel.'
    – Mick Doyle.

2. 'If we meet France five times, they'll beat us nine times out of ten.'
    – George Hook.

3. 'Cork has not had a Taoiseach since Jack Lynch. If [Declan] Kidney were not so busy, he would get elected in a landslide.'
    – George Hook.

4. 'It was a good match, which could have gone either way
    and very nearly did.'
    – Jim Sherwin.

NO ROOM FOR AMBIGUITY

Closer to home we have had a few classic quotes also. A particular favourite of mine is Dick West's 'I'd rather crawl across broken glass naked than speak to Will Carling.'

A MOUTHFUL

Although they revere *Sunday Times* columnist and former English international Stuart Barnes in Bath, they see him slightly differently in Wales.

The Welsh love telling the story of when Barnes was going to Llanfairpwllgwyngyllgogerychwyrndrobwllllantysiliogogogoch R.F.C. to speak at a gentlemen's evening. As he was driving up, he called into a café, and said to the waitress, 'Can you tell me where I am, but speak very slowly?' The waitress puckered up her lips and said 'Burrrrrgerrrrr King.'

Rugby Made Simple

Rugby is a technical game with its own specialised vocabulary. Many people do not fully appreciate the nuances of rugby speak. The following glossary of terms may help readers to understand this book more easily.

When a pundit says:
This wonderfully historic ground.
What the pundit really means is:
It's a proper dump.

When a pundit says:
You have to admire his loyalty to the club.
What the pundit really means is:
No other club would take him.

When a pundit says:
Few players show such flair.
What the pundit really means is:
He is a complete show-off.

When a pundit says:
He's a player who relies on instinct.
What the pundit really means is:
He hasn't a brain in his head.

When a pundit says:
This match was not without its moments.
What the pundit really means is:
It would have been more exciting to watch the TV with the screen shut off.

When a pundit says:
He has an interesting temperament.
What the pundit really means is:
He's a complete nutcase.

When a pundit says:
He shows great economy around the ball.
What the pundit really means is:
He never gets near the thing.

When a pundit says:
And the longstanding servant.
What the pundit really means is:
He must be entitled to free bus travel soon.

When a pundit says:
He's like a big jigsaw.
What the pundit really means is:
He falls to pieces.

When a pundit says:
You have to admire his competitive spirit.
What the pundit really means is:
He's a psychopath.

When a pundit says:
He's a seasoned veteran.
What the pundit really means is:
He's past it.

When a pundit says:
He showed great promise as a teenager.
What the pundit really means is:
He is totally useless now.

When a pundit says:
The referee had a poor view of the incident.
What the pundit really means is:
The ref is as blind as a bat.

When a pundit says:
He has a distinctive look.
What the pundit really means is:
He has a face only his mother could love.